Sports Law in Trinidad and Tobago

Sports Law in Trinidad and Tobago

J. Tyrone Marcus

This book was originally published as a monograph in the International Encyclopaedia of Laws/Sports Law.

Founding Editor: Roger Blanpain
General Editor: Frank Hendrickx
Volume Editor: Michele Colucci

Wolters Kluwer

Published by:
Kluwer Law International B.V.
PO Box 316
2400 AH Alphen aan den Rijn
The Netherlands
E-mail: international-sales@wolterskluwer.com
Website: lrus.wolterskluwer.com

Sold and distributed in North, Central and South America by:
Wolters Kluwer Legal & Regulatory U.S.
7201 McKinney Circle
Frederick, MD 21704
United States of America
Email: customer.service@wolterskluwer.com

Sold and distributed in all other countries by:
Air Business Subscriptions
Rockwood House
Haywards Heath
West Sussex
RH16 3DH
United Kingdom
Email: international-customerservice@wolterskluwer.com

Printed on acid-free paper

ISBN 978-94-035-2032-2

e-Book: ISBN 978-94-035-2034-6
web-PDF: ISBN 978-94-035-2040-7

Printed in the United Kingdom.

The Author

J. Tyrone Marcus is an Attorney-at-Law admitted to practice in Trinidad and Tobago, Jamaica and Barbados, an adjunct lecturer in Sports Law at the University of the West Indies (UWI), St. Augustine, Trinidad and a member of the North and Central America and the Caribbean Volleyball Legal Commission. He was a former board member of the Caribbean Regional Anti-Doping Organisation, a past legal adviser at the Ministry of Sport and Youth Affairs and a past Chairman of the Disciplinary Committee of the Trinidad and Tobago Professional Football League. He previously served as the legal consultant for Caribbean Association of National Olympic Committees Broadcasting Inc., the Caribbean media rights holders for the Rio 2016 Olympics and has been specialising in Sports Law since 2006. He has a Master's Degree in Sports Law and Practice from the De Montfort University in Leicester, England and is the co-author of *Commonwealth Caribbean Sports Law* (1st edn, Routledge, 2019). He has also published contemporary sports law articles for the *International Bar Association*, the *International Sports Law Journal*, the *Sport and the Law Journal*, the *World Sports Advocate*, the *Law in Sport* online journal and the *Global Sports Law and Taxation Reports*. He currently serves as the President of the Trinidad and Tobago Association for Sport and Law.

The Author

Acknowledgements

I wish to thank Professor Michele Colucci and Mr Joeri Lauwers for their helpful and consistent guidance throughout the editing and publication process. I also extend my gratitude to Professor Dr Ian Blackshaw for his review of the early sections of the monograph and to Dr Justin Koo, my co-lecturer in Sports Law at the Faculty of Law, UWI, St. Augustine, Trinidad, for his review of the sections on Intellectual Property. Special thanks are extended to my colleagues at the Trinidad and Tobago Association for Sport and Law, Mr Ricardo Williams, Ms. Sushilla Jadoonanan and Mr Stefan Fabien for their feedback and recommendations as they reviewed the remaining parts of the monograph.

Last, but by no means least, I thank my wife Michelle Marcus for her unfailing support and prayers through my time of study, research and writing.

Table of Contents

List of Abbreviations

ADR	Alternative Dispute Resolution
ADRV	Anti-doping Rule Violation
AIOWF	Association of International Olympic Winter Sports Federations
APMU	Athlete Passport Management Unit
ASATT	Amateur Swimming Association of Trinidad and Tobago
BCCI	Board of Control for Cricket in India
CAC	Central Audit Committee
CARICOM	Caribbean Community
CAS	Court of Arbitration for Sport
CAZOVA	Caribbean Zonal Volleyball Association
CBA	Collective Bargaining Agreement
CDRC	Cricket Dispute Resolution Council
CJEU	Court of Justice of the European Union
COE	Centre of Excellence
CONCACAF	Confederation of North, Central American and Caribbean Association Football
CPA	Cricket Players Association
CPL	Caribbean Premier League
CWC	Cricket World Cup
CWI	Cricket West Indies
CYG	Commonwealth Youth Games
DRC	Dispute Resolution Chamber
DTF	Danish Tennis Federation
ECHR	European Convention on Human Rights
EEC	European Economic Community
EU	European Union
FAPL	Football Association Premier League
FFA	Football Federation Australia

List of Abbreviations

FIFA	Fédération Internationale de Football Associations
FIVB	Fédération Internationale de Volleyball
FNASS	National Federation of Sportspersons' Associations and Unions
IAAF	International Association of Athletics Federations
ICAS	International Council of Arbitration for Sport
ICC	International Cricket Council
IDI	ICC Developmental (International) Limited
IOC	International Olympic Committee
IRC	Independent Review Committee
ISE	International Standard for Education
ISF	International Sports Federation
MHA	Methylhexaneamine
MLS	Major League Soccer's
MOU	Memorandum of Understanding
MSHSAA	Missouri State High School Activities Association
MSYA	Ministry of Sport and Youth Affairs
NAAATT	National Association of Athletics Administration of Trinidad and Tobago
NADO	National Anti-doping Organization
NBFTT	National Basketball Federation of Trinidad and Tobago
NCAA	National Collegiate Athletic Association
NKCTT	National Kickboxing Council of Trinidad and Tobago
NOC	National Olympic Committee
NORCECA	North and Central America and the Caribbean
NGB	National Governing Body
NSO	National Sporting Organisation
NSP	National Sports Policy
NZC	New Zealand Cricket
ODI	One Day International
OECS	Organisation of Eastern Caribbean States
OHIM	Office for Harmonisation in the Internal Market
OHSAA	Ohio High School Athletic Association
PE	Physical Education
PKATT	Point Kickboxing Association of Trinidad and Tobago
RTP	Registered Testing Pool
SCOTT	Sports Commission of Trinidad and Tobago
SGB	Sports Governing Body
SIGA	Sport Integrity Global Alliance

SPORTT	The Sports Company of Trinidad and Tobago
SSFL	Secondary Schools Football League
TFEU	Treaty on the Functioning of the European Union
TKR	Trinbago Knight Riders
TTABA	Trinidad and Tobago Amateur Boxing Association
TTADO	Trinidad and Tobago Anti-doping Organization
TTCB	Trinidad and Tobago Cricket Board
TTFA	Trinidad and Tobago Football Association
TTFF	Trinidad and Tobago Football Federation
TTGF	Trinidad and Tobago Gymnastics Federation
TTOC	Trinidad and Tobago Olympic Committee
TTPC	Trinidad and Tobago Paralympic Committee
TTKA	Trinidad and Tobago Karate Association
TTKF	Trinidad and Tobago Karate Federation
TTKU	Trinidad and Tobago Karate Union
TTWA	Trinidad and Tobago Wrestling Association
TUE	Therapeutic Use Exemption
TTVF	Trinidad and Tobago Volleyball Federation
UNESCO	United Nations Educational, Scientific and Cultural Organization
UWI	University of the West Indies
WADA	World Anti-doping Agency
WADC	World Anti-doping Code
WAKO	World Association of Kickboxing Organizations
WATT	Wushu Association of Trinidad and Tobago
WICB	West Indies Cricket Board
WIPA	West Indies Players Association
WIPO	World Intellectual Property Organization

List of Abbreviations

General Introduction

Chapter 1. General Background

1. In the seventy years from 1948 to 2018, Trinidad and Tobago has evolved as a genuine force in Caribbean sport, with consistent success at the international level in particular disciplines. Ince has noted:

> In 1948, when Trinidad accepted the invitation to participate at the Olympics in London, several sporting giants had already passed their prime. Francis Dinzey, Bobs Donowa, the Farrell brothers, Reggie and Teddy, Prince Dedier and Sergeant Bynoe, all trackmen, were already off the scene, as were cyclists Mikey Cipriani, Ahamad Charles, and Laurie Rogers. Some, who were too early to be in contention for the 1948 Games, had the opportunity to represent the colony at international meets in Europe.[1]

2. Making its Olympic debut in 1948, this twin-island Republic with just over 1.3 million inhabitants has witnessed a maturing of its sports sector while lamenting the missed opportunities for even greater progress from the grassroots to the elite level. Sport in 2019 and beyond, therefore, holds great promise for this tiny nation.

3. While most of the names quoted by Ince above are unlikely to match the fame of their later compatriots like Brian Lara, Dwight Yorke, Hasely Crawford, Gizelle Salandy, Ato Boldon, Shaka Hislop or Keshorn Walcott, those early Olympic participants symbolise the value of sport to a country that only gained its independence from British colonial rule in 1962. More than fifty-six years on from that historic Independence Day on 31 August 1962, sport in Trinidad and Tobago has managed to maintain an upward trajectory in keeping with general global trends, especially in the area of sports business, marketing and commerce. It is here that the law has made an inevitable intervention into sport's domain.

4. As Trinidad and Tobago sets its sights on the upcoming decade (2020–2030), the sports industry is poised to play a significant role in national development. As

1. Basil A. Ince, *Trinidad and Tobago at the Olympic Games: From Rodney Wilkes to George Bovell III* 17 (RPL(1991)LTD 2005).

a country that has been traditionally dependent on the oil and gas sectors as its primary revenue stream, the dramatic drop in global oil prices within recent years has forced the country to explore alternative means of earning revenue.

5. Sports tourism has been identified as one of those alternatives, therefore raising the stakes for each sport event the country hosts. New lenses, then, are being cast on themes like event bidding and event legacy, facilities management, the commercialisation of intellectual property rights, the negotiation of naming rights agreements and the exploitation of sports broadcasting rights. These considerations have taken on added value given the recent fluctuations in the Trinidad and Tobago economy.

6. Evidently, the time is opportune for the law to make its mark on the practice and delivery of sport in Trinidad and Tobago. It is anticipated that the local legislature and judiciary will play a pivotal role as the relationship between sport and the law continues to blossom.

§1. The Approach to This Monograph

7. Throughout the course of this monograph, particular emphasis will be placed on three of the leading National Governing Bodies (NGB)[2] for sport in Trinidad and Tobago:

(1) the Trinidad and Tobago Football Association (TTFA);[3]
(2) the Trinidad and Tobago Cricket Board (TTCB); and
(3) the National Association of Athletics Administration of Trinidad and Tobago (NAAATT).

8. The rationale for the focus on these three NGBs is that they all have had a rich legal and regulatory history and at the same time have also represented three of the country's most successful sports. By way of illustration, in the sport of football, administered by the TTFA, Trinidad and Tobago became only the second country from the English-speaking Caribbean to qualify for the senior men's Fédération Internationale de Football Associations (FIFA) World Cup when it did so in 2006 in Germany. In fact, up until the 2018 World Cup in Russia, Trinidad and Tobago was the smallest country to ever qualify for the event. However, Iceland, through its qualification for Russia 2018, now holds that record boasting a tiny population of less than 350,000 people.

9. Further, the sport of track and field, governed by the NAAATT, has provided Trinidad and Tobago with fifteen of its nineteen Olympic medals, including gold

2. The term 'National Governing Body' may be used interchangeably with the terms 'National Federation', 'National Sporting Organisation' or 'Sports Governing Body' in this monograph.
3. Also known as the TTFF.

medals from Hasely Crawford in 1976[4] and Keshorn Walcott in 2012,[5] the other four medals coming in swimming[6] and weightlifting.[7] In cricket, the current world-record holder for the highest individual score in test cricket and first-class cricket is Brian Lara of Trinidad and Tobago scoring 400 not out and 501 not out respectively.

10. Against this backdrop, this monograph will offer a detailed analysis of how the law has impacted on the administration of these three Sports Governing Bodies (SGBs) in particular, while comparisons with other governing bodies in Trinidad and Tobago will be made where the topic under consideration warrants it.

4. In the 100 metre sprint in Montreal, Canada.
5. In the javelin throw in London, England.
6. George Bovell won a bronze medal for Trinidad and Tobago at the 2004 Athens Summer Olympics.
7. Rodney Wilkes won a silver medal in weightlifting (featherweight category) at the 1948 London Olympics and followed that with a bronze medal in the same sport in the 1952 Helsinki Olympics. Lennox Kilgour also won a bronze medal for Trinidad and Tobago in weightlifting (middle heavyweight category) at the 1952 Olympics.

Chapter 2. Sources of Sports Law

11. The ongoing academic debate between advocates for sports law as its own discrete arm of the law, on the one hand, and those who maintain that 'sport and the law' more accurately reflects reality, on the other hand, will continue to run its course. In Trinidad and Tobago, the issue has little or no traction simply because this area of legal study and practice is still developing, although there is little resistance to the concept of there being an overlap between the law and sport. A definition of terms may aid in the discussion.

§1. Defining Sports Law

12. Author Mark James has noted that 'UK law has no formal definition of sport and consequently no formal definition of sports law … The quest for a definition of sports law is complicated further by ongoing debates about the most appropriate name for the subject and the proliferation of sub-names and sub-branches that have been claimed for it.'[8]

13. His analysis of the difficulty in defining 'sports law' is noteworthy. He resolved that dilemma by suggesting that the way to define sports law is by identifying 'the various sources of sports law and the jurisprudence that each is developing'.[9] This approach will be adopted in this chapter when seeking to ascertain the sources of sports law in Trinidad and Tobago.

14. Beloff's perspectives are also quite useful as he noted that the 'growth of legalism in sport is borne out of a desire for higher standards of justice, demanded by the sporting community as a consequence of the rise of professionalism and the increase in earnings potential within sport'.[10] Beloff here appears to identify if not the sources of sports law, at the very least, its roots: the desire for high standards of sporting justice, the rise of professionalism and the increase in earnings potential. These three concepts are intertwined and provide a common narrative in the international arena.

15. Yet, the question as to the sources of sports law is fundamental to a proper understanding of this fast-growing area of academic study. James' definitions stand out within sports legal scholarship and will be used to assess the sources of sports law in Trinidad and Tobago.

---

8. Mark James, *Sports Law* 3 (Palgrave Law Masters 3rd ed. 2017).
9. *Ibid.*, at 6.
10. Michael Beloff et al., *Sports Law* 10 (Hart Publishing 2d ed. 2012).

§2. Domestic Sports Law

16. James has defined domestic sports law as 'the creation of an autonomous legal order by a sport's national governing body (NGB) to regulate the conduct of its members and those playing its sport; it is the body of internally applicable law and procedure that has been developed by each sport's NGB'.[11] In this definition the role of the NGB is central. It is the NGB that has developed the regulations, law and procedure that are followed by its members and with which they must comply.

17. It is a generally accepted rule of sports governance that in every country, only one NGB is recognised for each sport. This reality, which reflects the pyramid structure of sport, and which also has competition law implications, means that the NGB in question has remarkable influence in charting the legal direction of its respective sport.

18. In Trinidad and Tobago, approximately fifty NGBs are recognised by the Ministry with responsibility for sport as having sole jurisdiction over the governance of that particular sport. The immediate consequence of this fact is that the development of domestic sports law has around fifty different channels although there will be expected overlap of common legal principles especially in the area of administrative law and its emphasis on natural justice, for instance.

§3. National Sports Law

19. James noted that in 'contrast to domestic sports law, national sports law is the development of a body of law and legal principles that is applied directly to sport by Parliament and the judiciary'.[12] National sports law, then, is heavily dependent on the decisions of the High Court of Trinidad and Tobago and the passage of sports-related Acts of Parliament.

20. There is a dearth of sports-based case law in Trinidad and Tobago although those who have been ventilated in the High Court have tended to have a degree of national prominence and public interest. In April 2017, Justice Frank Seepersad delivered a preliminary ruling arising from an Olympic team selection dispute in the lead up to the Rio 2016 Summer Olympics. In *Thema Williams v. The Trinidad and Tobago Gymnastics Federation, Marquez, Wattley, Lue Shue and Lue Shue,*[13] the question before Seepersad J. was whether the High Court proceedings should have been stayed to allow the dispute to be settled instead by arbitration. Ultimately, the stay was refused, but the law relating to Trinidad and Tobago sport was advanced.

---

11. James, *supra* n. 8, at 9.
12. *Ibid.*, at 11.
13. *Thema Williams v. The Trinidad and Tobago Gymnastics Federation*, Marquez, Wattley, Lue Shue and Lue Shue-Claim No. CV 2016-02608.

21. Crucially, Seepersad J. held the view that the public interest element to the case was strong enough that it warranted full determination in the courts. Some of his observations are worthy of mention given the multifaceted considerations that he weighed:

> The issues in this matter are of national importance. Given the unprecedented levels of crime and general sense of unease that confronts this nation, sports and the participation by athletes in international events instill a much needed sense of national pride and is one of the few avenues by which the flames of patriotism are fanned. Due to the pursuit of insular concerns, a prevailing sense of selfishness and complacency is very evident in this society and, as a consequence, mediocrity is often rewarded. This society is too blessed and has extensive unrealised talent for such a state of affairs to continue. There is a need to disregard bias, ethnic and/or political agendas, and there should be a resolve to ensure that only those who are most deserving are entrusted with the responsibility to make decisions and to represent us in all areas of national life.[14]

22. This was not an exaggerated view or an inflated assessment of the value of that case in the public sphere. It was the first time in the history of the Olympic Games that Trinidad and Tobago would have qualified a gymnast to the event. The fact that the two competitors, Thema Williams, the Claimant, and Marisa Dick, were of different ethnic backgrounds introduced a very sensitive and delicate dimension to the team selection controversy. Seepersad J., without using those words, saw his role in the development of national sports law as too significant to let arbitration decide the outcome. The final ruling, in this case, was delivered on 26 November 2018 and will be examined in greater detail in Chapter 3 of Part I.

23. The Trinidad and Tobago Parliament has rarely intervened in the regulation of sport. One of the earliest sports-related statutes was the 1933 Boxing Control Act which came into force on 1 January 1934. This Act established the Trinidad Boxing Board of Control and had the simple goal of being a statute passed to regulate the holding of boxing contests. Notably, recent discussions have been held within the sporting fraternity[15] with a view to repealing the Boxing Control Act in order to make way for the Combat Sports Act, a statute which has in view the regulation of boxing, kickboxing and mixed martial arts, three high-risk sports in terms of serious injury or death.

24. Outside of a few statutes incorporating some of the more popular local NGBs, including the incorporation of the country's National Olympic Committee (NOC) by way of the 1995 Trinidad and Tobago Olympic Committee (TTOC)

---

14. *Ibid.*, at para. 22.
15. 'Ministry of Sport Hosts Combat Sports Consultations', 4 Nov. 2017 http://www.looptt.com/content/ministry-sport-hosts-combat-sport-consultation.

(Incorporation) Act, perhaps only two other Acts of Parliament are of note: The 1988 Sport and Culture Fund Act[16] and the 2013 Anti-doping in Sport Act.[17]

25. The latter Act[18] was fully proclaimed by the country's President on 1 June 2015, but at the time of writing, no official governing board had been put in place. The former Act was not intended to be prescriptive legislation from a governance perspective but merely sought to establish a source of financial support for sporting and cultural initiatives.

26. It would be hard, therefore, to make a case for any meaningful Parliamentary influence on the development of national sports law in Trinidad and Tobago.

§4. Transnational Sports Law

27. James has stated that the 'link between domestic and national sports law is replicated at the transnational level by the relationships between global sports law and European and international sports law'.[19] He further defines European sports law as 'the law generated by the institutions of the EU and the explanations of how and why that law has been applied to sport in the decisions of the Court of Justice of the European Union (CJEU), and will continue to have an impact on UK law regardless of whether or not the UK remains a member state of the EU'.[20]

28. While Trinidad and Tobago obviously is not a member of the European Union (EU), there is an analogous context at the level of the Caribbean Community more popularly known as CARICOM, a group comprising of twenty countries in the Caribbean.[21] A second regional integration movement within the Caribbean is the Organisation of Eastern Caribbean States (OECS).[22] Adopting James' formula, transnational sports law in the Caribbean will refer to the law generated by CARICOM and/or OECS institutions and how that law has been applied to the practice of sport in the Caribbean.

29. There is no established field of law in the Caribbean known as CARICOM Law or OECS Law, but the law of the region has already been influenced by the rulings of the Caribbean Court of Justice and the interpretation of provisions of the Revised Treaty of Chaguaramas and the Revised Treaty of Basseterre. In *Caribbean Integration Law*, Berry has noted that although 'Caribbean integration has its

16. Act No. 31 of 1988.
17. Act No. 10 of 2013.
18. This Act will be analysed in detail in Part III of this book.
19. James, *supra* n. 8, at 14.
20. *Ibid.*
21. CARICOM currently comprises fifteen full members and five associate members. *See* https://www.caricom.org/.
22. The OECS began with seven member countries which signed the Treaty of Basseterre in 1981. The OECS now has nine members, https://eeas.europa.eu/headquarters/headquarters-homepage_en/4117/OrganisationEasternCaribbeanStates.

own unique organizations, organs, and processes, it must be remembered that the legal rules of CARICOM and OECS are grounded in public international law and the law of international institutions. Both regional organizations are founded upon treaties, and these constituent instruments are governed by the customary international law of treaties.'[23]

30. He also acknowledged the comparative benefit of EU Law on regional jurisprudence identifying what he called 'striking parallels.[24]' He added:

> There are, for example, clear similarities in the texts of the EU and Caribbean treaties. In some cases, the wordings of the treaty articles are almost, or are, identical. This is no accident. Caribbean legal drafters did not reinvent the wheel. Rather, they carefully selected and incorporated into their own treaties useful phrases and concepts which have evolved in the EU system.[25]

31. By way of example, Articles 45 and 46(1) of the Revised Treaty of Chaguaramas contemplate the free movement of workers, including sportsmen and sportswomen as follows. Article 45 stipulates: 'Member States commit themselves to the goal of free movement of their nationals within the Community.' Article 46 expands on this by establishing the agreement among the Member States 'to accord to the following categories of Community nationals the right to seek employment in their jurisdictions:

(a) University graduates
(b) media workers
(c) *sportspersons*
(d) artistes; and
(e) musicians …' [Emphasis added]

32. The seeds of transnational sports law, therefore, have been sown but the fruit is still a few years off from being borne in Trinidad and Tobago and the wider Caribbean.

§5. Global Sports Law

33. 'Global sports law' James has proposed 'aspires to be an autonomous transnational legal order created by the private bodies that govern sport at the world level … As with domestic sports law, global sports law is the body of internally applicable law and procedure that has been developed by each ISF[26] through the

23. David Berry, *Caribbean Integration Law* 3 (Oxford 2014).
24. *Ibid.*, p. 4.
25. *Ibid.*
26. International Sports Federation.

operation of the tribunals to which it allows disputes affecting their sports to be submitted'.[27] The role of International Sports Federations (ISFs)[28] is foundational to the development of global sports law. As a result of the contractual relationship that exists between each NGB and its counterpart ISF, there is an inevitably strong influence of the law developed by the latter on the legal framework of the former.

34. In Trinidad and Tobago, predictably, the impact of three ISFs has been the most significant: FIFA,[29] the International Cricket Council (ICC)[30] and the International Association of Athletics Federations (IAAF)[31] the latter's influence being most pronounced through its Anti-doping and Competition Rules. In the case of FIFA and the ICC, their footprint would have been most conspicuous during the hosting in Trinidad and Tobago of respective World Cups, namely the FIFA Under-17 Men's World Cup in 2001, the FIFA Under-17 Women's World Cup in 2010 and the ICC Cricket World Cup (CWC) 2007. With regard to the CWC, Trinidad and Tobago was one of nine host countries in the West Indies providing an opportunity for the regulations of the ICC to leave a stamp on the legal framework of that event.

35. It would be unconvincing to suggest that there was any significant evolution of global sports law during the three aforementioned events that led to some sort of development of domestic sports law. However, the mere fact that the then Trinidad and Tobago Football Federation (TTFF) would have been mandated during the youth world cups to comply with a Hosting Agreement containing detailed stipulations on matters, such as ambush marketing, ticket touting, broadcasting rights and the protection of FIFA's intellectual property rights, meant that the regulations of the ISF carried much weight at the local level. The cricket context was even more intricate since the Parliament of Trinidad and Tobago, like many of its neighbouring host countries, was compelled to enact 'sunset legislation' known as the ICC Cricket World Cup 2007 Act 2006[32] citing similar objectives as the FIFA Hosting Agreement. Again, these are just the planting of seeds with no immediate expectation of a harvest.

§6. International Sports Law

36. Perhaps it is this sub-category of sports law that has attracted the most attention from academics in this field. James has defined international sports law as 'the general or universal principles of law, particularly of international law, that are applicable to sport'.[33] Foster succinctly observed that since international law addresses the relationship between sovereign nations, then international sports law

27. James, *supra* n. 8, at 10.
28. ISFs are also commonly referred to as international federations, international governing bodies or world governing bodies.
29. FIFA, the world governing body for association football.
30. The ICC, the world governing body for cricket.
31. The International Association of Athletics Federations, the world governing body for track and field.
32. This statute will be analysed in detail in Part IV of this book.
33. James, *supra* n. 8, at 20.

'can be defined as the principles of international law applicable to sport'.[34] Foster himself cited Nafziger who held the view that 'as an authoritative process of decision-making and legal discipline, international sports law is as much a matter of international law as of sports law'.[35]

37. As a source of sports law, then, international sports law offers both authority and credibility if one accepts the submission that this branch of the law represents the principles of international law applied to sport. The implication is that the roots of international sports law may be found both in private international and public international law and that some of the most respected global legal authorities already have contributed and will continue to contribute to its development. It begs the question of whether an international agreement such as the 2005 United Nations Educational, Scientific and Cultural Organization (UNESCO) International Convention against Doping in Sport constitutes international sports law per se.

38. A related question also would be whether Trinidad and Tobago's ratification of that Convention in March 2007 represents the adoption of international sports law into its local jurisprudence. As a dualist nation, the 2005 UN Convention could only gain the force of law in Trinidad and Tobago via the enactment of local legislation which occurred on 1 June 2015 when the 2013 Anti-doping in Sport Act, mentioned earlier in this chapter, was fully proclaimed in the Trinidad and Tobago Parliament. This may very well be a case of at least a dual source of sports law, namely, national sports law and international sports law in Trinidad and Tobago. It is an issue worth exploring.[36]

§7. Sports Law Education

39. It is worth mentioning briefly that sports law education in Trinidad and Tobago has been growing within recent years, as seen with the introduction of Commonwealth Caribbean Sports Law as a third year elective module in the LLB programme at the Faculty of Law, University of the West Indies (the UWI), St. Augustine, Trinidad. This module now exists in addition to the Law and Sport modules which are also taught at the UWI, Trinidad campus, as part of the undergraduate degree in Sports Management and the UWI/FIFA/CIES[37] postgraduate diploma in Sports Management.

34. Ken Foster, *Is there a Global Sports Law? Lex Sportiva: What is Sports Law?* 37 (Robert C.R. Siekmann & Janwillem Soek ed., Springer 2012).
35. *Ibid.*
36. For an introductory overview of international sports law, *see* Prof Dr Ian Blackshaw, *International Sports Law: An Introductory Guide* (Asser Press 2017).
37. The International Centre for Sports Studies (CIES).

§8. Conclusion

40. As an independent nation of over fifty-five years, Trinidad and Tobago is at a special place in its maturity on many levels, including on the legal landscape. The birth of sports law is yet another manifestation of this country's journey to developed status as it seeks to join the global academic discussion of a fascinating and evolving area of law.

Chapter 3. The Specificity of Sport

41. The 2009 Treaty of Lisbon brought relief and optimism to the European sporting community:

> The Union shall contribute to the promotion of European sporting issues, while taking account of the specific nature of sport, its structures based on voluntary activity and its social and educational function.[38]

42. For the first time, the EU had been given some express competence in the field of sport. However, there is no equivalent provision in the Caribbean.

43. The question as to whether sport needed to be treated specially and to benefit from the well-known 'sporting exemption' has been debated for over forty years from the days of *Walrave & Koch v. Union Cycliste Internationale (UCI)*[39] and *Donà v. Mantero.*[40] Gardiner noted that, even before these two landmark cases in the mid-1970s, the EU, formerly called the European Economic Community (EEC), 'was not granted any specific competence in the field of sport at its inception by the Treaty of Rome in 1957'.[41] It was in *Walrave*, in particular, that the question of the applicability of Community law to sport gained traction. *Walrave*, a case which was eventually referred to the European Court of Justice under what was then Article 177 of the EEC Treaty (Article 267 of the Treaty on the Functioning of the European Union (TFEU)), sought to answer various questions, including what was the basis, if any, on which sport fell within the terms of the Treaty.

44. One of the key findings of the Court of Justice was as follows: 'Having regard to the objectives of the Community, the practice of sport is subject to Community law only in so far as it constitutes an economic activity within the meaning of Article 2 of the Treaty.'[42] This principle has been tried, tested and restated for decades. Gardiner admitted that the Court's willingness to accept that purely sporting rules of a non-economic nature, such as rules concerning the selection of national teams, were effectively outside the scope of the Treaty has become a contentious principle.[43]

45. Caribbean territories have not had either the benefit of the academic or the practical discussion surrounding the special nature of sport. The evolution of sports law in Trinidad and Tobago has occurred with an understanding of sport's social, health, economic and educational benefits, yet sport's specificity has not ever been on the policy, research or political agendas.

---

38. Article 165 (1), TFEU.
39. Case C-36/74, [1974] ECR 1405.
40. Case C-13/76, [1976] ECR 1333.
41. Simon Gardiner et al., *Sports Law* 143 (Routledge 4th ed. 2011).
42. At para. 4 of the ruling.
43. Gardiner, *supra*, n. 41.

46. The consequence of this is that sports governance in Trinidad and Tobago does not reflect the philosophy that sport is unique and should be treated differently from other sectors and industries. What does exist is the pyramidal structure of sport, which is inevitable given the contractual nature of the relationship between National Federations and the parent International Federations on the global stage.

47. Football, arguably the most popular sport in Trinidad and Tobago, offers a useful example of how the sporting pyramid exists with FIFA being the world governing body, Confederation of North, Central American and Caribbean Association Football (CONCACAF) being the continental federation, the Caribbean Football Union being the regional association and the TTFA[44] being the SGB. This situation is clearly not unique to Trinidad and Tobago, nor is it unique to the sport of football, but is indicative of the monopoly that is a natural outflow of the sporting pyramid. Consequently, this makes sport unique in a limited sense and, perhaps, is the only true manifestation of the specificity of sport in Trinidad and Tobago.

48. Potentially, monopolistic structures in other industries would be condemned, discouraged or outlawed by Competition Commissions pursuant to competition law, but sport appears to be offered concessions especially since it is one of the few industries where the elimination of your competitors is actually unhealthy. For example, W Connection Football Club, a perennial title contender in the Trinidad and Tobago Professional Football League (TT Pro League), welcomes competition from other teams like Central United FC, the Defence Force or St. Ann's Rangers. In the absence of these rivals, there would be no league and no product to be consumed by sports fans. This applies across the globe in myriad sports. This, too, renders sport unique and lends credence to the advocacy of those who submit that the specificity of sport demands that sport be treated in a special way.

49. It took a long time, through Article 165 of the 2009 Lisbon Treaty, before the European Commission was given competence over sport, which many commentators believe was still only a limited one. In the foreseeable future, it is not anticipated that there will be any treaties in the nature of the Revised Treaty of Chaguaramas (which, incidentally, was adopted in Trinidad and Tobago) that will impact on the administration of sport in the Caribbean, whether directly or indirectly. However, sport will continue to be special for fans and administrators in Trinidad and Tobago, if only for its uncanny ability to bring ephemeral euphoria, national pride, goodwill and unity in a way that few other endeavours can.

---

44. A more detailed analysis of the TTFA will take place in Part I of the text, under the theme 'The Organization of Sport.'

Part I. The Organisation of Sport

Chapter 1. Sports Policy

50. Under the guidance of the Australian Sports Commission, Trinidad and Tobago launched its first National Sports Policy (NSP) in 2002 (NSP 2002) with a two-pronged emphasis on High Performance Sport and Total Participation in Sport. It was a timely policy, drafted in clear language and articulating specific functions for multiple stakeholders. The 2002 National Sports Policy (NSP 2002), therefore, was a tangible manifestation of years upon years of laying a foundation and erecting the first few layers of a sporting structure that would hopefully stand the test of time.

51. Unlike the 2007 European Union (EU) White Paper on Sport, which like various European Community (EC) Treaties, gave an increasing competence to the European Commission and Court of Justice to intervene in sport, NSP 2002 did not contemplate such a relationship. The involvement of law and legal bodies in sport was simply not in view.

52. More recently, the Government of the Republic of Trinidad and Tobago launched a successor policy, the 2017–2027 National Sport Policy (NSP 2017), which proposed a bespoke Tobago Sport Policy as an Appendix.[45] The 2017 policy embraced the role of the law, highlighting legislative reform as a significant feature of the development of sport in the future.

§1. The NSP 2002: An Historic Initiative

53. The introduction to the NSP 2002 offers helpful context in understanding the genesis of the policy. It recognised that in 'Trinidad and Tobago there have been many plans and programmes to develop sport in the past and some of these efforts may have, directly or indirectly, borne fruit internationally in certain team and individual sports. However there was always the popular opinion that sport lacked: (i)

45. Tobago is the second island in this twin-island Republic and has a population of about 61000 people.

A proper policy; and (ii) The required resources to facilitate its development in the context of its increasing scientific, competitive and professional nature internationally.'[46]

54. The policy drafters, then, took notice of the absence of both a proper policy and adequate resources to promote the development of sport in the context of a rapidly evolving global industry. Notably, the consultative process necessarily involved the input of various NGBs, referred to in the NSP 2002 both as National Sport Associations and as National Sporting Organisations (NSOs).

55. The NSP 2002 sought to capture the generally accepted rule that each sport should be represented by one NGB locally. With a few exceptions, sport in Trinidad and Tobago, generally, has remained faithful to this principle, notwithstanding the potential competition law implications that may flow from an abuse of this monopolistic position.[47]

56. Commendably, the NSP 2002 articulated the value of women's sport, listing as one of its objectives the encouragement of full participation of women and girls in sport, pursuant to the 1994 Brighton Declaration on Women and Sport.[48] It will be seen subsequently, though, that women's sport in Trinidad and Tobago has continued to struggle to obtain adequate investment, advocacy and media exposure that would guarantee its sustainability.

57. The legal component of the NSP 2002 was admittedly a limited one, with brief mentions of doping control in Article 13 and arbitration mechanisms in Article 15. Article 15 stated that An Arbitration Council would be established pursuant to the National Sport Management Commission Act, with the council being an independent body that had the 'primary function of settling disputes in a manner adapted to the specific needs of the sports world and consistent with the Code of Sports-Related Arbitration adopted by the Court of Arbitration for Sport (CAS) and the International Council of Arbitration for Sport (ICAS)'. Since 2002, neither has the National Sport Management Commission Act been passed nor has the Arbitration Council been established. There have been preliminary discussions at the state level, however, about the creation of the Sports Commission of Trinidad and Tobago (SCOTT).[49]

§2. The NSP 2017

58. Fifteen years after the creation of the NSP 2002, the Government of Trinidad and Tobago finalised a successor policy called the National Policy on Sport

46. *2002 National Sports Policy*, 3.
47. This theme will be addresses in greater detail in Ch. 2 of Part 1.
48. Page 5.
49. 'National Sports Commission to replace SPORTT'-Joel Bailey, 4 Oct. 2017, https://newsday.co.tt/2017/10/04/national-sports-commission-to-replace-sportt/.

2017–2027 (the NSP 2017). It was officially adopted in March 2018[50] and launched in September 2018.[51] The need for an updated policy was uncontested in sporting circles, with stakeholders cognisant of the vast difference that fifteen years had made in the sporting landscape internationally and locally.

59. Richard Parrish's perspective, in a European context, appears to have local relevance in Trinidad and Tobago when he suggested that, in view of the parallel juridification and commercialisation of sport, a sports policy is primarily regulatory in nature although it still seeks to acknowledge both the cultural and social features of the industry.[52] The NSP 2017 reflects this reality.

60. The NSP 2017 also encompassed a twin-theme, based on the similarly named concepts of Development of Sport and Sport for Development. The policy *values*[53] are centred on:

(a) Integrity
(b) Democracy
(c) Commitment
(d) Achievement of Excellence
(e) Tolerance
(f) Fair Play
(g) Respect.

61. The policy identifies six core *principles*[54]:

(1) Equity
(2) Co-operation
(3) Productivity
(4) Sustainability
(5) Transparency
(6) Validity.

62. These values and principles have been placed within a broader context of twelve major *goals*[55]:

(1) clarifying the roles and responsibilities of sport organisations;
(2) improving overall governance;
(3) improving financial management;

50. 'National Sports Policy launched in Parliament'-Newsday, 17 Mar. 2018, https://newsday.co.tt/2018/03/17/national-sports-policy-launched-in-parliament/.
51. 'Official Launch of the National Sport Policy (2017–2027)', http://www.news.gov.tt/content/official-launch-national-policy-sport-2017-2027#.XAkp9WhKiM8.
52. Richard Parrish, *Sports Law and Policy in the European Union* 6 (European Policy Research Unit Series, Manchester University Press 2003).
53. *National Sports Policy 2017–2027*, at 20.
54. *Ibid.*, at 21–22.
55. *Ibid.*, at 28.

(4) promotion of sport specific research development and planning;
(5) improvement of asset management and infrastructural development;
(6) promotion of public private partnerships;
(7) development of the sport tourism sector;
(8) addressing the deficiencies and shortages of human resource and technical skill within the sport industry;
(9) prioritising sport marketing, promotion and communication;
(10) developing sport commerce;
(11) promoting sport as a tool for social development; and
(12) adopting comprehensive sport development system and focus.

63. It is noteworthy that the objectives of the NSP 2017 included the improvement of governance, the development of sport commerce and the prioritisation of sports marketing. This is where juridification and commercialisation meet each other. While NSP 2002 did identify as one of its objectives the facilitation of the development of sport as an industry that would in turn enhance an athlete's earning capacity and boost the national economy, the language of the NSP 2017 is more definitive and specific in this regard.

64. The stipulation of Legislative Reform and Institutional Reform as strategic dimensions to support the dual themes of Development of Sport and Sport for Development, is particularly striking, especially given the vision that the following pieces of legislation and/or legislative policies would be earmarked:

(1) The Sport Act
(2) Legislation establishing:
    (a) The Sport Commission
    (b) The Sports Disputes Tribunal and
    (c) The Combat Sports Commission[56]
(3) The Major Events Management Act
(4) Child Protection in sport legislation
(5) A Sport Governance Policy regarding the management of National Governing Bodies
(6) Legislation regarding the implementation of a Sport Complaints Authority.

65. Exciting possibilities exist in Trinidad and Tobago with respect to the future administration, regulation and management of sport. The challenge, as is often the case, is to move from policy-setting to implementation.

66. Policy formulation has also been on the agenda of global umbrella organisations. In May 2016, Mrs. Louise Martin CBE, Chair of the Commonwealth Advisory Board on Sport urged Commonwealth Member States to support the efforts of the Commonwealth Sports Movement and the Commonwealth Youth Sport for

56. The proposed Combat Sports Act has been earmarked to repeal the Boxing Control Act of 1933.

Development and Peace 'in order to further position sport as an important consideration in central policy debate and national development planning'.[57] Such admonitions are welcome as they foster interdependence among stakeholders with common interests and goals.

67. The Caribbean region is one of those geographical clusters of territories that reap the benefits of proximity, community and shared vision. It was therefore not surprising that the journey to the adoption of NSP 2017–2027 involved a helpful comparison with neighbouring policies, the most recent of which emanated from Jamaica in 2013.

§3. Conclusion

68. As an independent nation of over fifty-five years, Trinidad and Tobago is at a special place in its maturity on many levels, including on the legal landscape. The birth of sports law is yet another manifestation of this country's journey to developed status as it seeks to join the global academic discussion of a fascinating and evolving area of law.

57. Chair's Statement, 24 May 2016, Commonwealth Advisory Board on Sport.

Chapter 2. Sports Governance

§1. Governmental Bodies and Institutions

I. The Ministry of Sport and Youth Affairs

69. The Government Ministry with responsibility for sport in Trinidad and Tobago is the Ministry of Sport and Youth Affairs (MSYA). This Ministry over the years has partnered with other sectors such as education, culture and community development and back in 2015 it moved from being solely the Ministry of Sport to becoming, not for the first time, the Ministry of Sport and Youth Affairs (hereinafter called 'the MSYA').

70. The MSYA, at present, is one of twenty-three Ministries of Government currently led by the political party known as the People's National Movement. Before 2015, the ruling political party was the People's Partnership, whose primary and largest political entity was the United National Congress. As happens with any political cycle in most territories, some policies change when Governments change.

71. After the general elections of September 2015, the incoming Government articulated its vision for sport envisioning that 'as many citizens as possible should be involved in Sports and Recreation and that Trinidad and Tobago must strive to be a world class sporting nation satisfying local, regional and international needs while providing sustainable employment and contributing to national wellbeing'.[58] This vision embraces five sub-themes, namely:

(1) wide participation in sport and recreation;
(2) being a world-class sporting nation;
(3) satisfying needs at the local, regional and international levels;
(4) providing sustainable employment; and
(5) contributing to national well-being.

72. This five-fold statement of intent is distilled even further by identifying almost thirty specific ways in which the Government of Trinidad and Tobago, through the MSYA, in particular, would accomplish these objectives. Each method is succinctly stated in the Manifesto and, because of its importance in delivering sport services in Trinidad and Tobago, the complete array is listed below without further expansion:

– increase the pool of talent from which world champions can emerge for international recognition;
– promote sports as a way to curb crime and build social skills;
– use sport to reduce the high incidence of chronic lifestyle diseases prevalent in the country;

58. 2015 Manifesto of the People's National Movement at p. 62.

- use sport to foster greater communication and understanding amongst different communities, races and creeds in the country;
- use sport as a means of dealing with aggression and other forms of youth delinquency in communities and schools in the country;
- increase sports involvement in educational institutions, in particular, primary schools;
- inculcate a physical education (PE) programme for all educational levels and increase the hours allocated to sport and recreational activities each week;
- improve the transportation system to sporting facilities and events;
- foster greater diversity and improve the quality of community sporting programmes to capture the skills of people within these communities;
- improve the availability of physical therapy;
- increase participation opportunities for underrepresented groups in particular disabled persons, women, girls and the vulnerable youth and improve physical facilities to cater for this targeted group of persons;
- develop an advocacy programme which would not only highlight the need for total participation but will also stress on improvement of mental, social, spiritual and financial benefits that can be derived from an active lifestyle;
- improve the availability of information of sports involvement by conducting a National Sport and Recreational Census;
- create an online information pool to allow easy access to sporting information and schedule of various activities throughout the country;
- emphasise the growth of an effective Athlete Development System by empowering people to adopt the 'cradle to grave' development of an athlete;
- foster and develop involvement in sport in schools at all levels by encouraging and supporting inter-school competitions across Trinidad and Tobago;
- offer tax incentives to private and other interest groups to adopt amateur community sporting clubs;
- promote Trinidad and Tobago as an attractive location for major international sporting events;
- actively develop and promote sports tourism;
- promote marine sporting activities;
- provide incentives for the growth and development of professions allied to sport, such as sports medicine, physical therapy and sports media;
- similar to what Jamaica has done successfully, develop Trinidad and Tobago as a sporting brand and form strategic alliances with countries and organisations to enhance penetration into the international sports market;
- develop a formalised talent identification and recruitment scheme and establish a sports marketing mechanism to promote sports locally;
- develop and promote a range of activities to maximise facility usage and commercial return.
- develop a Domestic Sport Research Database by performing a bi-annual survey which will establish benchmarks, improvements to the local sports industry and provide comprehensive data for sports and recreation locally;

– encourage industry creativity and development by cultivating innovative strategies to create career opportunities and an apprenticeship system for skills acquisition and research initiatives towards creating marketable products for building the Sports Industry;
– improve sports infrastructure and facilities across the country, ensuring it is up to the highest international best standards;
– offer local athletes workshops on how to speak to the media and to become a Public Relations Officer of local sports; and
– create a Sports Institute of Trinidad and Tobago that will capture and hone the skills of young athletes while growing and modernising the sports industry.[59]

73. The aforementioned list of implementation measures has been incorporated into the NSP 2017, under which this country expressed an intention to establish, via an Act of Parliament, the SCOTT which, once created, would either restructure or replace the Sports Company of Trinidad and Tobago (SPORTT).[60]

II. The Sports Company of Trinidad and Tobago

74. The 'SPORTT' was incorporated in September 2004 pursuant to the Companies Act Chapter 81:01. SPORTT is one of a number of Special Purpose State Enterprises in Trinidad and Tobago which have been established as implementing agencies on behalf of specific line ministries. The line ministry for SPORTT is the MSYA, with the latter focusing on setting policy guidelines and the former taking charge of implementation of that policy.

75. It must be admitted, however, that clear lines of demarcation have not been easy to identify from time to time as the MSYA and SPORTT have sought to complement each other's work and functions. In its earliest days, SPORTT was charged with responsibility of overseeing the operations and governance of only a handful of sports. The rationale, commendably, was to focus on a few sports so that they could receive sufficient attention, in terms of technical and financial support and the grant of human and capital resources.

76. Eventually, the number of sports overseen by SPORTT grew to sixteen. The rationale for this expansion still seems to be a matter of contention within administrative circles and views are mixed as to whether SPORTT's oversight of the increased number of disciplines has been reflected in greater success in those sixteen sports.[61]

59. *Ibid.*, at pp. 62–64.
60. Joel Bailey, '*National Sports Commission to replace SPORTT*', Trinidad and Tobago Newsday, 4 Oct. 2017, https://newsday.co.tt/2017/10/04/national-sports-commission-to-replace-sportt/.
61. At the time of writing, the number of NGBs overseen by SPORTT was reduced to fifteen, namely, basketball, amateur/Olympic boxing, cricket, cycling, football, golf, gymnastics, hockey, netball, rugby, sailing, swimming, tennis, track and field and volleyball.

77. In a situation that is not unique to Trinidad and Tobago, there is often a battle for who should get the credit for the success of a sport from a podium-finish perspective. From the standpoint of major prizes on the global stage, track and field stands out as the most successful sport in Trinidad and Tobago's history with fifteen of the nineteen Olympic medals won by this country, belonging to track and field. The only two Olympic gold medals have come in this discipline, with Hasely Crawford winning the 100 metre gold in Montreal, Canada in 1976 and then teenager Keshorn Walcott producing, arguably, one of the biggest upsets ever in Olympic field events by winning the men's javelin throw in London 2012.

78. Track and field is one of the disciplines overseen by SPORTT but since it is an Olympic sport, there is a significant preparatory function to be played by this country's NOC, the TTOC. Yet, even more directly involved on a day-to-day basis is the NGB for track and field, the NAAATT. At the same time, the MSYA is the primary funder of most sports in Trinidad and Tobago and assists the TTOC in offsetting the cost of travel in getting teams to the Olympics or the Commonwealth Games, for instance.

79. While the question of who gets the credit really is insignificant in the wider scheme of things, it sometimes has a greater effect than it should because it impacts on the investment each of the stakeholders would make if they all are concerned about whether there is a tangible return on that investment. What makes the track and field context more interesting is that the NAAATT is one of the few NGBs in Trinidad and Tobago that has not been heavily dependent on financial support from the state due to successful corporate partnerships with Adidas for a number of years, Puma at present, and the National Gas Company of Trinidad and Tobago, to name a few.

80. While this backdrop has not made SPORTT's role redundant, on occasion, questions have been raised as to whether overlapping administrative functions such as facilities management and oversight of NGBs which are often performed by Government entities have reduced both effectiveness and efficiency in the delivery of sport services.

III. The Trinidad Boxing Board of Control

81. Established by statute as the Trinidad Boxing Board of Control, the Trinidad *and Tobago* Boxing Board of Control, (as it is more commonly known and which is hereinafter called 'the Boxing Board'), has existed for around eighty-five years. The Boxing Control Act Chapter 21:52 was passed in 1933 and come into force on 1 January 1934. The Boxing Board was given the authority to regulate the holding of boxing contests. Yet, as amateur boxing started to emerge in the late 1940s and early 1950s, the question being asked at that time was whether the Boxing Control Act was intended to regulate only professional boxing or should have included amateur boxing as well. The question has never really been settled.

82. According to section (2)1 of the Boxing Control Act, the Board will have a minimum of five persons, namely, a Chairman and no less than four others. These appointments are made by the Minister with responsibility for sport. The very fact of ministerial appointments creates a tense and sometimes volatile environment with tensions often brewing between the Board and the Trinidad and Tobago Boxing Association.[62] The ambiguity surrounding the scope of the Boxing Board's powers can easily raise concerns about whether there is state interference in the administration of local boxing.

83. The wording of sections 7(1) and 9 demonstrates the uncertainty. Section 7(1) (a) states as follows: 'The Board may prescribe the Rules for boxing and may from time to time amend or revoke any such Rules, and with the approval of the Minister may make Regulations as to all or any of the following matters: (a) the registration and licensing and the revocation or suspension of licences of- (i) promoters of *professional* boxing contexts; (ii) *professional* boxers; (iii) *professional* seconds; (iv) referees, judges and timekeepers; (v) premises in which boxing contests may be held.' [Emphasis added]

84. The language of section 7(1) (a) suggests that the type of boxing activity contemplated is professional boxing. Yet, section 9 of the Boxing Control Act states that the 'Board may by permit in writing either generally or in respect of any specific context exempt any scholastic institution or any a*mateur* athletic or any other organised association or body from all or any of the provisions of this Act or any Regulations made thereunder and may in its discretion revoke any such permit.' [Emphasis added].

85. The implication here is that an amateur sporting body including an entity governing amateur boxing has to submit to the jurisdiction of the Boxing Board regarding the receipt of a permit to hold an event. Indeed, the subsequent birth of the Trinidad and Tobago Amateur Boxing Association (TTABA) brought this statutory consideration to life and in practice, the TTABA has always sought written permission from the Boxing Board to host amateur boxing contests.

86. Notwithstanding the aforementioned ambiguity in discerning the intent of the legislative drafters, in practical terms, no real confusion existed once the TTABA was established. That body oversaw amateur boxing while the Boxing Board regulated professional boxing.

87. The waters were muddied, however, in or around the time of the 2012 London Summer Olympics when the International Boxing Association mandated its member federations globally to remove the word 'amateur' from their names. For this country, it meant that the TTABA now became the Trinidad and Tobago Boxing Association (TTBA). More significantly though, from a governance perspective, it left practitioners in the country confused as to whether there were now two bodies governing professional boxing in Trinidad and Tobago. The recent sojourn of the

62. Formerly the Trinidad and Tobago Amateur Boxing Association.

World Boxing Council into amateur boxing on the international stage has only exacerbated the confusion. It is hoped that if the Combat Sports Act is eventually passed, it would provide an opportunity to clarify roles and functions not only in boxing but also in other combat sports captured under that proposed legislation.

§2. NOC and Sports Governing Bodies

I. The TTOC (Incorporation Act) 1995

88. The TTOC is the NOC for Trinidad and Tobago. Pursuant to the Trinidad and Tobago Olympic Committee (Incorporation) Act 1995 (The TTOC Incorporation Act),[63] the TTOC was established as a body corporate and was given the mandate to affiliate with the International Olympic Committee (IOC) and to comply with and enforce the rules and regulations of the IOC.[64] These IOC rules are enshrined in its constitutional document, the Olympic Charter, which is often updated or amended in or around September in any given year where changes are needed. At the time of writing the applicable edition of the Olympic Charter was the version that came into force on 9 October 2018.

89. The TTOC has authority over the participation of national teams in events sanctioned by the IOC, including the Olympic Games, the Commonwealth Games, the Pan American Games and the Central American and Caribbean (CAC) Games.[65] The TTOC also seeks to offer financial assistance, through fundraisers or otherwise, to teams attending the foregoing Games.

II. The Constitution of the TTOC

90. Operating in tandem with the TTOC Incorporation Act as a governance document is the TTOC constitution, the most recent edition of which was adopted in April 2018. In its constitution, the TTOC describes itself as a 'non-governmental and not-for-profit organisation of unlimited duration'.[66] Taken together with its corporate personality, the legal nature of the TTOC mirrors other NOCs and/or associations of NOCs on the global stage, such as the European Olympic Committees and the Association of National Olympic Committees which both describe themselves as not-for-profit non-governmental organisations, albeit under Swiss law instead.

91. One of the more significant recent developments in the constitutional history of the TTOC was the amendment made in April 2018 in response to complaints that the arbitral process could only be triggered by sports governing bodies

63. Act No. 29 of 1995.
64. *Ibid.*, at s. 3.
65. *Ibid.*, at s. 3(b).
66. Article 1.

and not by other parties, such as clubs or individual athletes. This came to a head in *Rheann Chung and Dexter St. Louis v. Trinidad and Tobago Table Tennis Association.*[67] In this case, veteran table tennis player Dexter St. Louis and his step-daughter Rheann Chung challenged his non-selection for the 2018 Gold Coast, Australia Commonwealth Games. Of significance in this case was the fact that it forced a change in the TTOC's constitution, wherein the arbitral process could be commenced by an athlete. Up until *St. Louis v. TTTTA* only sporting organisations could start the process. The wording of the arbitration clause of the constitution pre-*St. Louis* was as follows:

> All affiliated National Sporting Organisations may submit to the Trinidad and Tobago Olympic Committee for settlement all disputes/conflicts within their Organisation, which such Organisations deems to be unresolved, subject to their respective constitutions and subject to the rules of their respective International Federations to which they are affiliated.[68]

92. The effect of Article 31.1 as it was then drafted was to allow only the NSOs to submit a dispute to the TTOC for settlement. It was the NSO that had the power to bring the dispute to the TTOC if, in its view, the conflict remained unresolved. It did not matter if an individual sportsman or sportswoman had a dispute to be resolved. If the NSO did not raise the issue as a matter for resolution, the individual was left with no recourse before the TTOC. On this issue, the court noted as follows: 'The wording of the TTOC constitution is such that it leaves it to the discretion of member Associations whether to refer disputes for arbitration. Even though such disputes may involve individual sports persons there is no means for the individual sportsman or woman to raise a dispute with the TTOC directly – as with all their other dealings with the TTOC; they must do so through their national association.'[69]

93. Things changed after the commencement of the *St. Louis* case. Article 31, the arbitration provision, now reads as follows:

> All affiliated National Sports Organisations or their registered members may submit to the Trinidad and Tobago Olympic Committee for settlement all disputes/conflicts which may be deemed to be unresolved, subject to their respective constitutions and subject to the rules of their respective International Federations to which they are affiliated.

94. The amended Article 31 now includes the phrase 'or their registered members'. The breadth of potential complainants, therefore, has been broadened to

67. CV 2017-04608.
68. Article 31.1, 2016 TTOC Constitution.
69. *Rheann Chung and Dexter St. Louis v. Trinidad and Tobago Table Tennis Association*- CV 2017-04608, at para. 10.

include registered members of the NSO. Depending on the extent of the membership categories of the NSO, there could now be an additional two, three or even more layers of disputants triggering the arbitration clause.

95. Incidentally, St. Louis himself was the first to invoke the expanded Article 31 when in June 2018 he was again omitted from the national table tennis team, this time with respect to the Central American and Caribbean Games (CAC) Games which were held in Barranquilla, Colombia from 19 July to 3 August 2018. The consequence of that arbitration was that no men's team was selected to represent Trinidad and Tobago at those Games.[70] It is anticipated that the revised Article 31 may very well open the proverbial 'flood gates' regarding disputes being submitted to the TTOC since the scope of potential claimants has been widened.

III. The TTOC as the Local Arbiter of Sporting Disputes

96. It was worth noting that the foregoing Article 31 arbitration clause identifies the TTOC as the local arbiter of sports-related disputes among its registered members. The Council of the TTOC will select no more than three arbitrators whose decision may first be appealed to an Appeals Tribunal also appointed by the TTOC with a final appeal to the CAS.[71]

97. The absence of an independent sports-specific dispute resolution body in Trinidad and Tobago is often magnified when disputes are submitted to the TTOC. This is a potential strain on the TTOC's resources which are already stretched by the fact that it also acts as the de facto National Anti-doping Organisation (NADO) for the country due to there being no board appointed to the Trinidad and Tobago Anti-doping Organization (TTADO).

98. It is hoped that the TTOC would eventually be freed up to concentrate on preparing teams for the various multisport Games under its purview, once the gaps are filled in the dispute resolution and anti-doping realms in Trinidad and Tobago.

IV. The Affiliates of the TTOC

99. As is the case with other NOCs, the sports that appear on the summer Olympic programme dominate the list of Olympic affiliates in Trinidad and Tobago. The following sports governing bodies are affiliated with the TTOC:

- The National Association of Athletics Administration
- The National Ballroom Dance Association of Trinidad and Tobago
- The Trinidad and Tobago Badminton Association

70. Derek Achong, *Another Legal Tennis Win for St. Louis*, Trinidad Guardian, http://m.guardian.co.tt/sports/2018-07-10/another-legal-tennis-win-for-st-louis, 10 Jul. 2018.
71. Article 31.2 and 31.5, TTOC Constitution adopted on 28 Apr. 2018.

- The National Basketball Federation of Trinidad and Tobago
- The Trinidad and Tobago Boxing Association
- The Trinidad and Tobago Canoe/Kayak Association
- The Trinidad and Tobago Chess Association
- The Trinidad and Tobago Contract Bridge Association
- The Trinidad and Tobago Cricket Board
- The Trinidad and Tobago Cue Sports Foundation
- The Trinidad and Tobago Cycling Federation
- The Trinidad and Tobago Darts Association
- The Trinidad and Tobago Equestrian Association
- The Trinidad and Tobago Football Association
- The Trinidad and Tobago Gymnastics Federation
- The Trinidad and Tobago Hockey Board
- The Trinidad and Tobago Judo Association
- The Trinidad and Tobago Karate Union
- The Trinidad and Tobago Netball Association
- The Trinidad and Tobago Paralympic Committee
- The National Pigeon Racing Commission of Trinidad and Tobago
- The Trinidad Rifle Association
- The Trinidad and Tobago Rugby Football Union
- The Trinidad and Tobago Sailing Association
- The Trinidad and Tobago Sports Medicine Association
- The Trinidad and Tobago Squash Association
- The Amateur Swimming Association of Trinidad and Tobago
- The Trinidad and Tobago Table Tennis Association
- The Trinidad and Tobago Taekwondo Association
- The Trinidad and Tobago Target Archery Federation
- The Trinidad and Tobago Team Handball Association
- The Tennis Association of Trinidad and Tobago
- The Trinidad and Tobago Triathlon Association
- The Trinidad and Tobago Volleyball Federation
- The Trinidad and Tobago Weightlifting Association
- The Wushu Association of Trinidad and Tobago.

100. Interestingly, the above-mentioned list of affiliates includes two bodies, which are themselves umbrella bodies, namely, the Trinidad and Tobago Paralympic Committee (TTPC) and the Trinidad and Tobago Sports Medicine Association, an entity comprising sports medicine professionals. The other thirty-four affiliates are bona fide NGBs. Incredibly, around 50% of those thirty-four NGBs are known to have had legal battles and/or governance challenges that were either ventilated in the courts of law, were settled before litigation or became the subject of media attention.

101. Towards the end of 2018, a legal threat appeared to be looming in the tennis fraternity as the parents of teenager David Rodriguez gave notice of their intention to appeal to the TTOC following a declaration from the Tennis Association of

Trinidad and Tobago that Rodriguez was ineligible for selection to the 2019 Under-16 Junior Davis Cup qualifying tournament.[72] At the time of writing no formal procedure had been initiated before the TTOC.

V. The Legal Status and Constitutional Framework of National Governing Bodies in Olympic and Non-Olympic Sports

102. It is not surprising that when one takes a panoramic view of the landscape of sports governing bodies in Trinidad and Tobago, that one finds a fairly even mix of entities that are unincorporated associations and others that have attained legal personality either through a private Act of Parliament or pursuant to the Companies Act Chapter 81:01.

103. As with the TTOC, the following private Acts established the respective sporting organisations as bodies corporate:

- The Trinidad and Tobago Cricket Board of Control (Incorporation) Act, No. 34 of 1989 which was amended by the Trinidad and Tobago Cricket Board (Incorporation) (Amendment) Act, No. 13 of 2001.
- The Trinidad Rifle Association (Incorporation) Act, No. 27 of 1975.
- The Trinidad and Tobago Yachting Association (Incorporation) Act, No. 44 of 1975.
- The Trinidad and Tobago Wrestling Association (Incorporation) Act, No. 39 of 1977.
- The Trinidad and Tobago Netball Association (Incorporation) Act, No. 29 of 1979.
- Trinidad and Tobago Football Association (Incorporation) Act, No. 17 of 1982.
- Trinidad and Tobago Special Olympics (Incorporation) Act, No. 13 of 1991.
- Trinidad and Tobago Secondary Schools Football League (Incorporation) Act, No. 19 of 1995.

104. There was an attempt in 2009 to enact the TTFF Bill, but evidently, it did not progress. A few aspects of that Bill are worthy of mention.

105. The short title of the proposed legislation named the statute as the Trinidad and Tobago Football Federation (Incorporation) Act 2009.[73] Clause 2 of the Bill accorded the TTFF legal corporate personality while Clause 3 listed three primary objectives:

72. Ian Prescott, *Tennis Tension-Rodriguez Seeks TTOC Intervention for Junior Davis Cup berth*, Trinidad Express, https://www.trinidadexpress.com/sports/local/tennis-tension/article_946a5228-0aff-11e9-8ae9-cff0c3a998ab.html, 28 Dec. 2018.

73. No. 18 of 2009.

(1) to regulate and control the conduct of football in Trinidad and Tobago (under the FIFA) and to provide playing fields and conveniences in connection therewith;

(2) to promote local, inter-territorial and international football matches and to provide prizes or awards to participants thereof; and

(3) to foster and promote the playing of football under the said system and to become members of or affiliated to associations having similar objectives.

106. Importantly, all rights, privileges, advantages, liabilities and obligations under the former TTFA would be transferred to the TTFF under Clause 5. Under Clause 10, the Trinidad and Tobago Football Association (Incorporation) Act 1982[74] would be repealed.

107. Although the 2009 Bill was never enacted, the TTFF still existed as its own independent body, notwithstanding the incorporation of the TTFA by an Act of Parliament in 1982. In other words, the TTFF was born even before the 2009 Bill, and although there was an intention to transfer all rights and liabilities of the TTFA to the TTFF under the 2009 legislation, it is unclear whether such a legal transfer actually did occur before 2009.

108. Interestingly, in its 2001 constitution, the TTFF, in Article 1, referred to itself as the TTFF, yet at the same time, stated that it was incorporated under the TTFA (Incorporation) Act 1982. After its incorporation in 1982, it is unclear exactly when the TTFA started to refer to itself as the TTFF. Had the 2009 Bill been passed, any existing ambiguities as to the legal status of either entity would have been removed but, prima facie, it appears that there never was any intention to create two separate bodies but that the TTFA and the TTFF would be one and the same organisation.

A. *Election Controversies and Constitutional Interpretation*

109. In March 2017, the Facebook page of the Wushu Association of Trinidad and Tobago (WATT)[75] contained the following disclaimer notice: 'The [W]ushu [A]ssociation of Trinidad and Tobago wishes to advise the public that Mr Rahman Khabir is no longer an Officer of the Association and is not authorised to conduct any transaction on our behalf.' For persons familiar with the Wushu Association, it would have been a well-known fact that the said Rahman Khabir was one of its long-standing Presidents.

110. A few months earlier, in August 2016, another Facebook post informed the public of the results of the WATT's general elections, naming Ronald Ramlochan as the President. Yet, in a media article in December 2016, Khabir was named as the

74. No. 17 of 1982.

75. The confusion was escalated due to the fact that around this time there were two Wushu Associations, each with separate Facebook pages and both using the same name.

WATT President.[76] Evidently, there was some fallout as to who was the duly elected President of WATT, culminating in the 2017 disclaimer notice. Such a scenario is neither new to sport nor unique to Trinidad and Tobago.

111. Back in 2008, the TTOC invoked a mediation process[77] to resolve a dispute within the National Basketball Federation of Trinidad and Tobago (NBFTT) concerning the lawfulness of the person appointed to be the Federation's President. The presidential contest was between Brian Manning and the late Earl John and revolved around the interpretation of Article 17 of the NBFTT's constitution which addressed the filling of vacancies and removal from office.[78] By the end of the mediation process, John was reinstated as NBFTT President, although the details of the confidential settlement agreement were leaked to the media.

112. The critical feature of the resolution of the NBFTT presidential dispute was the fact that an interpretation of the constitution assisted in bringing the matter to closure. Such is the value of NGBs having properly drafted constitutions.

VI. Constitutional Changes in Cricket, Football and Athletics

A. The Constitution of the TTCB

113. The three featured sports in this monograph have all had relatively recent constitutional changes with the TTCB doing so in 2013, the TTFA in 2015 and the NAAATT in 2016. Cricket, though, may be poised for changes in the near future given the new template provided to the TTCB as part of the February 2018 Kokaram Report.[79]

114. A significant proposal in the draft 2018 TTCB constitutional template is a change of name from the TTCB to Cricket Trinidad and Tobago. This would synergise well with the recently rebranded West Indies Cricket Board (WICB), which is now known as Cricket West Indies (CWI), and it would mirror other well-known cricket governing bodies such as Cricket Australia, Cricket South Africa and Cricket Zimbabwe.

115. In offering context for the proposed name change, the Independent Review Committee (IRC), chaired by Justice Vasheist Kokaram, observed that 'over the years the name of the body responsible for Trinidad and Tobago cricket has changed. The IRC views such changes in name as more than nominal and indeed

76. *Hypolite joins Wushu Kung Fu*, Trinidad Guardian, http://www.guardian.co.tt/sports/2016-12-19/hypolite-joins-wushu-kung-fu, 19 Dec. 2016.
77. Mediation and arbitration will be addressed in greater detail in Ch. 3 of Part I of this book.
78. Don Farrell, *John Back at Basketball Helm*, www.latinbasket.com, 15 Jun. 2018.
79. 'A Report on the Governance of Trinidad and Tobago Cricket'-IRC, 22 Feb. 2018 chaired by Justice Vasheist Kokaram. Dr. Sheila Rampersad and Mr. Ellis Lewis were the other two committee members.

reflective of a change in the overall approach and professionalism of the board'.[80] The past names of the TTCB were the Trinidad Cricket Council in 1956, the Trinidad and Tobago Cricket Council in 1958 and the TTCB of Control in 1980. It was in 2003 that the name Trinidad and Tobago Cricket Board was adopted. In the context of Caribbean sport, the removal of the word 'control' was a welcome initiative.

116. In fact the Kokaram Report, notably, goes as far as saying that 'the IRC is of the view that an important if not symbolic gesture must be made to demonstrate that cricket is larger than the organisation and that the organisation and governance structure is merely a vehicle to serve the larger interest of cricket and all that it symbolises'. That symbolic gesture would be the change of name to Cricket Trinidad and Tobago (CT&T).

117. Second, the 2018 TTCB constitutional template expands the 2013 constitution from thirty to forty articles. Some of the salient new proposed articles address the following themes:

(1) neutrality and non-discrimination;[81]
(2) promoting the spirit of the game;[82]
(3) term limits for directors;[83]
(4) the establishment of standing committees including an Ethics and Compliance Committee and a Legal Affairs and Intellectual Property Rights Committee.[84]

118. Additionally, a detailed section on dispute resolution has been proposed in the 2018 template with the formation of a Cricket Dispute Resolution Council (CDRC) as the principal internal entity appointed by the Board of CT&T. Within the dispute resolution structure are a Zonal Disciplinary Committee, a National Disciplinary Committee, a National Appeals Committee and a Tribunal which serves as the final level of appeal on all disciplinary matters.[85]

119. The IRC also envisioned that, once the CDRC has received a complaint or notice of dispute, it would refer these matters to either a Cricket Arbitration Council or a Cricket Mediation Council.[86] Notably, the IRC advocated that the dispute resolution processes should be exhausted before resort to the Court is sought.[87] This was not a suggestion that the jurisdiction of the court should be ousted but merely that litigation should not be the first course of action.

80. *Ibid.*, at p. 23.
81. Article 4.
82. Article 5.
83. Article 9.05.
84. Article 12.02.
85. Articles 26–28.
86. Kokaram Report, p. 66.
87. *Ibid.*

B. The Constitution of the TTFA

120. The landscape of local football has been both colourful and controversial. It meant that the July 2015 ratification of a new constitution was a welcome move, a process which, incidentally, was played out in the public domain. A high-profile team was assembled to spearhead that constitutional review including World Cup 2006 goalkeeper and ESPN football analyst Shaka Hislop, TTOC President Brian Lewis and Dinanath Ramnarine, former head of the West Indies Players' Association (WIPA), the representative body of West Indies cricketers.

121. The 2015 constitution contains eighty-three articles, which is indicative of the continued evolution of this governance document, given the fact that the 2001 constitution of the then-TTFF contained fifty-four articles. An earlier but undated draft constitution ('the undated constitution') of the TTFF contained forty-three articles. In the undated constitution, full membership in the TTFF was given to those associations that were 'properly constituted bodies playing football according to the laws of FIFA'.[88] No explanation was offered in that constitution as to what was necessary to qualify as a 'properly constituted body'.

122. By 2001, an interpretation clause was included which defined a 'properly constituted body' as 'any organisation, whether incorporated or not, engaged in the playing, promotion or administration of Association Football'. By 2015, that term was removed from the definition section. This was a reflection of the modernisation of the game.

123. Indeed, the 2015 revision of the TTFA constitution represented a high point for football governance in Trinidad and Tobago given the expertise that was accessed in the process. The end product was an impressive thirty-page, eighty-three-article document which encompassed key aspects of sports governance, management and administration.

124. The following represent some of the key provisions of the 2015 constitution:

(1) Neutrality and non-discrimination (Article 3).
(2) Compliance with the Laws of the Game as created by the International Football Association Board (Article 6).
(3) Judicial Bodies of the TTFA, namely the Disciplinary Committee, the Ethics Committee and the Appeal Committee.
(4) Detailed disciplinary measures (Article 64).
(5) The dispute resolution provisions addressing the role of the Arbitration Tribunal and the CAS. (Articles 65–67).

88. Article 5(a).

125. The disciplinary measures in Article 64 are noteworthy as they represent possibly the first time that the TTFA, and maybe even any NGB in Trinidad and Tobago, has included such a clear and specific provision on sanctions for disciplinary offences. Article 64 has been reproduced below in its entirety.

The disciplinary measures are primarily:

(1) for natural and legal persons:
  (a) a warning;
  (b) a reprimand;
  (c) a fine;
  (d) the return of awards.
(2) for natural persons:
  (a) a caution;
  (b) an expulsion;
  (c) a match suspension;
  (d) a ban from the dressing rooms and/or the substitutes' bench;
  (e) a ban from entering a stadium;
  (f) a ban on taking part in any football-related activity;
  (g) social work.
(3) for legal persons:
  (a) a transfer ban;
  (b) playing a match without spectators;
  (c) playing a match on neutral territory;
  (d) a ban on playing in a particular stadium;
  (e) annulment of the result of the match;
  (f) expulsion from a competition;
  (g) a forfeit;
  (h) deduction of points;
  (i) relegation to a lower division;
  (j) replaying a match.

126. When this detailed provision is compared to the undated TTFA constitution, the distinction is glaring. Article 39 of that constitution, entitled, 'Penalties' listed only four sanctions:

(1) a caution;
(2) a censure;
(3) a fine;
(4) suspension from all or any specific football activity, either permanently or for a stated period.

127. By 2001, the then-TTFF included a more advanced dispute resolution clause, which named an arbitration tribunal as the forum for dealing with disputes.[89] The article then stated that an arbitral award was 'a condition precedent to

89. Article 43 of the 2001 TTFF Constitution.

any right of action, whether seeking a declaration or injunction or any other order or determination against or liability of the Federation'.[90] In other words, before a party could seek legal redress from the courts, an attempt at Alternative Dispute Resolution (ADR) had to be made, specifically arbitration. This trend continued in 2015.

128. Article 65 of the 2015 constitution, the arbitration clause, like the 2018 constitutional template of the TTCB, raises the question of ousting the court's jurisdiction. Article 65 states: 'Disputes in the Association or disputes affecting Leagues, members of Leagues, Clubs, members of Clubs, Players, Officials and Officials of other Associations, shall not be submitted to Ordinary Courts, unless the FIFA regulations, this Constitution or binding legal provisions specifically provide for or stipulate recourse to Ordinary Courts.'

129. A party's access to the courts according to *Scott v. Avery*[91] is not contingent upon the grant of permission pursuant to an NGB's constitution. That is a common law right which cannot be ousted. At best, NGBs should encourage the exhaustion of internal remedies before access to the court is sought. Bypassing the courts cannot be a constitutional mandate and, if stated in such language, the relevant clause is likely to be struck off by a court of law as unlawful.

C. *The Constitution of the NAAATT*

130. The most current edition of the constitution of the NAAATT was adopted in October 2016, five years after its incorporation as a not-for-profit organisation pursuant to the 1995 Companies Act.[92] Modelled off of a constitutional template produced in 2009 by the MSYA but adapted to suit its own specific purposes, the 2016 NAAATT constitution includes welcome provisions on anti-doping, child protection, dispute resolution and agents. The fifty-two articles of the 2016 constitution depict an increase from the thirty-nine articles of the 2003 constitution.

131. For instance, Article 49.2 of the 2016 constitution in contemplating a role for sports agents stipulates that 'sportspersons must enter into written agreements with their agents, which agreements must adopt the rules, regulations and principles of the IAAF'. This clause represents an appreciation by the NAAATT for both the commercial and contractual reality of the modern-day sports industry, while it also seeks to acknowledge the expectation of compliance between any given NGB and its parent body.

132. Article 50 deals with anti-doping and places the responsibility on the NAAATT to adhere to the 2013 Anti-Doping in Sport Act,[93] while Article 51 is a

90. Article 43.4.
91. (1856) 5 HL Cas 811.
92. Ch. 81:01.
93. This Act will be examined in detail in Part III, Doping and Sport.

welcome inclusion calling on the NAAATT to adopt child protection policies that would safeguard vulnerable participants from the threat of any predators that may have infiltrated the sport. Article 48 is the Dispute Resolution clause which accords jurisdiction to an Internal Dispute Tribunal and which invokes both mediation and arbitration as part of the process to manage and resolve arising conflicts.

D. General Comment

133. The foregoing overview of the constitutions of the three NGBs that form the focal point of this monograph reveals similar trends. Certain provisions remain central to governance of the respective organisations and as a result, the passage of time yields no significant change in those clauses. These include:

(1) objects of the Association;
(2) affiliation to regional and international federations;
(3) membership categories, rights and obligations;
(4) the conduct of meetings, including Annual General, Extraordinary and Special General Meetings;
(5) officers of the association and their functions;
(6) amendment to the constitution.

134. On the other hand, there has been a consistent evolution of provisions addressing dispute resolution and disciplinary proceedings, generally speaking, bringing more sophistication to these clauses. The inclusion of new standing committees in the respective NGBs over time to cover matters like finance, marketing, doping, match-fixing, intellectual property rights and non-discrimination has been conspicuous, especially in the more experienced governing bodies in Trinidad and Tobago.

135. Barker and Stevens in their helpful text, *Club Law Manual,*[94] have identified the following clauses as basic in the drafting of a constitution for a club which, if sports-based, will itself be affiliated to an SGB:

(1) Name
(2) Aims and Objectives
(3) Membership
(4) Membership Fees
(5) Officers of the club
(6) Management Committee
(7) Finance
(8) Annual General Meetings
(9) Discipline and Appeals

---

94. Kerry Barker and Henry Stevens, *Club Law Manual* (Wildy, Simmonds & Hill Publishing 2d ed. 2011).

(10) Dissolution
(11) Amendments to the constitution
(12) Declaration or adoption of the constitution.[95]

VII. Notable Provisions from the Constitutions of Other National Governing Bodies in Trinidad and Tobago: A Snapshot

A. *Special Olympics of Trinidad and Tobago*

136. The standout clause from the 2009 constitution of Special Olympics of Trinidad and Tobago was Article XIII which expressly stated that its members were subject to the Laws of the Republic of Trinidad and Tobago as well as the Rules and Regulations of Special Olympics International and Special Olympics Caribbean. While it is understood that national law has supremacy over the internal sporting law of an SGB, it is rare to see an express provision endorsing same.

B. *National Kickboxing Council of Trinidad and Tobago*

137. Probably the most controversial clause in the 1997 constitution of the National Kickboxing Council of Trinidad and Tobago (NKCTT) was the provision stipulating the qualifications for any presidential candidate. The criteria included the following:

(1) the candidate must be a certified representative for a world governing body recognised by the National Kickboxing Council;
(2) the candidate must have experience in Full-contact, Kickboxing and Muay-thai;
(3) the candidate must be internationally trained in the procedures of management and must be familiar with the laws and business relating to kickboxing.[96]

138. At the time of writing, it was uncertain whether this provision remained intact in the most current edition of the constitution. Unsurprisingly, the clause was viewed as both controversial and restrictive as it seemed to eliminate most persons from the presidential race given the high bar that was set. Up to the year 2017, the founding president was apparently still the sitting president, twenty-six years after the birth of the NKCTT in 1991.

---

95. *Ibid.*, at pp. 183–187.
96. Page 14 of the 1997 constitution.

C. Trinidad and Tobago Automobile Sports Association

139. One of the notable provisions of an undated version of the constitution of the Trinidad and Tobago Automobile Sports Association was Article 24 which addressed the power of the Motor Sport General Council. One such power was that the General Council would act as an Appeal Board for members who have alleged that they have been the recipients of unfair treatment. Prima facie, the General Council is too big of a group to properly serve as an appellate body, and sports governance best practice suggests that a bespoke Appeals Committee comprising persons with the requisite competence, experience and qualifications should perform that function. It is not uncommon in Trinidad and Tobago for NGBs to grant such authority to a General Assembly or General Council.

D. Trinidad and Tobago Canoe/Kayak Federation

140. Article 25 of the constitution (undated) of the Trinidad and Tobago Canoe/Kayak Federation stood out, commendably, because of its express inclusion of para-athletes. Article 25.1 stated that the 'Federation shall be affiliated to the Trinidad and Tobago Paralympic Committee (TTPC) and shall adopt its rules, regulations, codes and bye-laws and any other and all documents relevant to the administration and governance of the TTPC.' Connected to this was Article 27.6, in the context of dispute resolution, in which unresolved disputes specifically relating to para-athletes would be submitted to the TTPC for arbitration.

E. Trinidad and Tobago Target Archery Federation

141. A surprisingly rare clause in the context of Trinidad and Tobago sport was Article 16 of the 2005 constitution of the Trinidad and Tobago Target Archery Federation. That article sought to regulate communication with the media in the following terms: 'No official, archer, referee or member of the Federation shall represent or criticise publicly the views of any of the Federation's business on the subject of target archery without the approval of the Executive Committee. Any person so offending shall be guilty of misconduct.'

142. The apparent intent behind such a clause is the protection of the image and reputation of the Federation. The means of achieving that goal is the regulation of communication which raises fundamental human rights questions, including the freedom of speech. The wording of the clause is unfortunate since it seems to be pursuing two related objectives:

(1) that no one under the jurisdiction of the Federation should represent its views without the approval of the Executive Committee; and
(2) that no one should publicly criticise the Federation or views articulated by the Federation.

143. It is with respect to the second item that freedom of speech questions can be raised. Other NGBs have sought to address this concern by incorporating the catch-all phrase of 'not bringing the Association into disrepute'.

F. Trinidad and Tobago Judo Association

144. One noteworthy provision of the constitution of the Trinidad and Tobago Judo Association is Article 55 which adopts Bye-Laws *in addition to* its Constitution. This is potentially a tricky question because of the overlapping terminology used to describe the governance documents of NGBs. In sports governance circles the following terms are commonplace:

(1) Constitution: referring to the supreme governance document of the sporting body, whether incorporated or not.
(2) Byelaws/By-laws: sometimes used as a synonym for constitution, rules or regulations.
(3) Company By-laws: referring to the governance documents that regulate the sporting body's existence as a company.
(4) Olympic Charter byelaws: referring to the explanatory notes annexed to respective Rules of the Olympic Charter.

145. Therefore, when the Judo Association identifies that it has byelaws appended to its constitution, closer scrutiny of the constitution reveals it is referring to company byelaws given its incorporation as a non-profit organisation in September 2003. The simple lesson is that NGB constitutions must use clear language when describing their regulatory documents.

G. Tennis Association of Trinidad and Tobago

146. The 1992 constitution of the Tennis Association of Trinidad and Tobago contained provisions that were impressively futuristic given the time of its drafting. Article 23 of that constitution was entitled 'Conditions Governing Players' with one such condition being the prohibition of advertising by any player within the precincts of a tournament, match or competition in which he is entered as a competitor, unless the rules of the International Tennis Federation provided otherwise. It is submitted that the commercial realities of sport in 1992 were markedly different than the current landscape so that the prevention of personal advertising appears positively anachronistic.

147. It is also worthy to note Article 23(b) of the said 1992 constitution which expressly stated that at a given time, any one tennis player could be subject to the jurisdiction of more than one National Tennis Association if playing in an event administered by a tennis association separate and apart from his home association. The article went on to say that if there were a conflict in the rules, then the rules of the other association would prevail. The clarity of the provisions belied its age.

H. Trinidad and Tobago Volleyball Federation

148. Volleyball is one of the sports where the contents of the constitutions from the apex to the base of the governance pyramid closely mirror each other. An examination of the constitutions of the Fédération Internationale de Volleyball,[97] North and Central America and the Caribbean,[98] Caribbean Zonal Volleyball Association[99] and the Trinidad and Tobago Volleyball Federation (TTVF) reflects the attempt at harmony.

149. However, early drafts of the TTVF's constitution, prior to the aforementioned increasing harmonisation, contained a useful provision offering details of player transfers, a clause more usually associated with association football. Article 5 of the 2007 version of the TTVF's constitution referred to the Certificate of Transfer and the fixed fee of USD 100.00 which likely represented an administrative cost rather than an expression of the transferring player's value.

I. Amateur Swimming Association of Trinidad and Tobago

150. Perhaps the most salient feature of this constitution is the name of the organisation. Arguably, the name 'Amateur Swimming Association of Trinidad and Tobago (ASATT)' can no longer be used to reflect accurately how much local swimming has evolved in the country.

151. A 1992 version of ASATT's constitution defined an amateur swimmer as 'one who engages in swimming solely for pleasure and the physical, mental and social benefits he derives therefrom and to whom swimming is nothing more than a recreation for which no remuneration is received'.[100] It is hard to juxtapose this definition with the swimming exploits of Trinidad and Tobago's 2004 Athens Olympic bronze medallist George Bovell or 2018 CAC Games triple gold medallist Dylan Carter, who also won a silver medal at the 2018 Gold Coast Commonwealth Games in Australia.

152. Both of these world-class swimmers would have been registered for the respective major events through the TTOC which not only serves as the NOC for Trinidad and Tobago but also as its Commonwealth Games Association, a normal practice for the small islands of the Caribbean. Yet, as part of the national selection process for the Olympics or the Commonwealth Games, it is the NGB that would have to submit names to the TTOC for final ratification. For swimming in Trinidad and Tobago, ASATT is the duly recognised NGB.

97. Federation Internationale de Volleyball, the sport's world governing body.
98. The North, Central American and Caribbean Volleyball Confederation, the sport's continental governing body for that geographical region.
99. The Caribbean Zonal Volleyball Association, one of the two zonal governing bodies for Caribbean volleyball, the other one being the Eastern Caribbean Volleyball Association.
100. Article 2 (Interpretation).

153. The solution seems to be a straightforward one. ASATT can follow the lead of the NAAA whose acronym originally stood for 'National Amateur Athletic Association' but now means 'National Association of Athletics Administrations'. Other NGBs internationally in various sports have had to make similar amendments to their names, notably in the sport of boxing. In Trinidad and Tobago, for instance, the TTABA became the TTBA. It is a simple case of keeping in step with the evolution of the sports industry.

VIII. One NGB per Sport

154. The 2002 National Sport Policy of Trinidad and Tobago articulated the well-established sports governance practice of there being only one NGB per sport per country. That practice is essentially rooted in contract law with each National Federation being contractually bound to its respective International Federation. Article 5.2 of the NSP 2002 states:

> There shall be one (1)National Sporting Organization for each individual sporting discipline. This Organization shall be recognized as the official body to administer the sport, based on the financial, administrative and organizational criteria established by the Ministry responsible for the development of Sport. National Sporting Organizations shall be autonomous bodies in matters relating to the administration of their sport. They shall have the sole right to select national teams to represent Trinidad and Tobago at Tournaments and Championships conducted under the jurisdiction and the recommended National Body of their respective International Federations.

155. While there has been a general adherence in Trinidad and Tobago to this principle, a few notable exceptions exist, some more controversial than others. The following three examples all emanate from the combat sports fraternity.

A. *Karate*

156. The martial arts family in Trinidad and Tobago is a fractured one with karate at the very heart of the divisions, not necessarily because of the personalities involved but especially because of the very layered nature of the sport. One consequence of the factions in karate has been the creation of three bodies with confusingly similar names:

(1) The Trinidad and Tobago Karate Union (TTKU);
(2) The Trinidad and Tobago Karate Federation (TTKF); and
(3) The Trinidad and Tobago Karate Association (TTKA).

157. To the untrained eye, any one of these bodies could be seen as the NGB given the use of the words 'Trinidad and Tobago' before each name. Evidently, only the TTKU is recognised by the TTOC and by the MSYA as the sport's NGB, but this has not prevented both confusion and acrimony within the sport, especially since the TTKF is very active and they both have similarly worded constitutions. The TTKA seems to be less public in its operations and appears only to have a presence on social media.[101]

158. From a legal standpoint, no known litigation has been commenced by the TTKU against its rival bodies, likely because the TTKU has no ongoing active trade or commercial activity that would warrant protection under the Trade Marks Act Chapter. 82:81. Similarly, there is no record that the World Intellectual Property Organization (WIPO)[102] Mediation and Arbitration Center has been approached to lodge a complaint about a confusingly similar domain name.

B. Wrestling

159. Wrestling in Trinidad and Tobago has a rich history, especially since it was one of the few sources of sports-based entertainment in the 1960s and 1970s. Further to the sport's popularity in that era, the Trinidad and Tobago Wrestling Association (Incorporation) Act 1977 was passed. According to section 2, it was created as a body corporate with perpetual succession. Section 3 gave it the power, *inter alia*, 'to promote and hold wrestling cards, rallies and *all wrestling sport activities* under the rules of Wrestling held under the International Sporting Code, the General Competition Rules and Standing Regulations of the Trinidad and Tobago Wrestling Association or other recognised wrestling authority and in connection therewith *to exercise all such powers* and to do all such things as are usual or incidental to the holding of such wrestling cards, rallies or other wrestling sport activities'. [Emphasis added]

160. The clear and unambiguous language of the incorporating legislation of the Trinidad and Tobago Wrestling Association (TTWA) points to an all-encompassing oversight over all wrestling activities in Trinidad and Tobago. This meant that the more recent creation of the Trinidad and Tobago Wrestling Federation would inevitably lead to conflicts between the two entities, although the parties have made attempts to co-exist by separating 'Olympic wrestling' from 'entertainment wrestling'. This distinction is yet to be tested and only time will tell whether these two similarly named bodies will be able to exist harmoniously and autonomously.

101. Generally speaking, especially with those sports on the Olympic programme, the Ministry of Sport would usually endorse the status of the NGB that is recognised by the TTOC and that is also affiliated with an International Federation that is recognised by the IOC.
102. WIPO.

C. Kickboxing

161. Kickboxing is the only sport in Trinidad and Tobago with two permitted governing bodies that exist in a non-controversial manner. That stems from the fact that it was the world governing body, the World Association of Kickboxing Organizations (WAKO), that made the dual appointment therefore granting NGB status to both entities, namely, the previously mentioned NKCTT and the Point Kickboxing Association of Trinidad and Tobago (PKATT).[103]

162. WAKO elected to appoint the NKCTT as the NGB for the ring sport aspect of kickboxing while PKATT was named as NGB for the mat or tatami aspects of kickboxing. These two bodies have worked without much tension over the years. However, the birth of the Trinidad and Tobago Kick Boxing Federation has caused some splintering in the fraternity. Nevertheless, there is no confusion as to whom WAKO recognises as its bona fide affiliates in Trinidad and Tobago.

§3. General Comment

163. Many of the NGBs in Trinidad and Tobago remain unincorporated associations. As a result, there has been no active intervention from the Companies Registry at the Ministry of the Attorney General and Legal Affairs with respect to the NGBs bearing similar names. Nevertheless, there still appears to be much room for applying greater scrutiny to the use of the name Trinidad and Tobago before the name of the given sporting body. Until, then, at the very least, stakeholder confusion and factious sporting relationships may very well characterise the day-to-day environment of some local sports.

§4. Sports Governance: Concluding Perspectives

164. In August 2018, the Association of International Olympic Winter Sports Federations (AIOWF) revealed its findings from what was its second governance review. It highlighted two main areas of weakness, namely, the lack of female representation and the general absence of term limits.[104] This AIOWF review served as a reminder that sports governance has emerged as one of the most topical and relevant sports law sub-themes in modern times.

---

103. Recently rebranded as the PKATT Sport Martial Arts Association.
104. Michael Pavitt, *Gender Balance and Term Limits Highlighted As Areas of Weakness in Second AIOWF Governance Review*, https://www.insidethegames.biz/articles/1069035/gender-balance-and-term-limits-highlighted-as-areas-of-weakness-in-second-aiowf-governance-review, 20 Aug. 2018.

165. Trinidad and Tobago has embraced the call to advance its own governance reforms, through umbrella bodies like the TTOC and one of its key affiliates, the NAAATT. In June 2018 TTOC President Brian Lewis[105] succinctly articulated the present challenges:

> Corruption is at the heart of the problems in local sport and hence the resistance to sport governance reform and modernisation. Attempts to put processes and policies in place that address corruption and malfeasance are resisted or sabotaged. Advocating for governance reform and ensuring transparency and accountability are meeting stiff resistance … Financial integrity and transparency are the cornerstones of good governance.[106]

166. The TTOC has provided solutions to these problems by establishing its own good governance code in 2016.

167. Back in 2011, former TTOC Vice President Ian Hypolite embarked on an analytical study of governance in the NAAATT as part of an Executive Master's Degree in Sports Organisation Management. Notably, in his recommendations for change, the question of term limits, among many others, was raised and this was supported with a broad proposal that best practice should be adopted from the Australian Sports Commission's Governance Principles. It remains to be seen whether there is sufficient administrative fortitude in Trinidad and Tobago to chart, in practical ways, a new pathway that culminates in sustainable sporting good governance.

105. At the time of writing Lewis was sitting as a member of the Executive Committee of the Sport Integrity Global Alliance.

106. Stephon Nicholas, *Lewis: Corruption Hindering Good Governance in Sport*, https://newsday.co.tt/2018/06/17/lewis-corruption-hindering-good-governance-in-sport/, 17 Jun. 2018.

Chapter 3. Dispute Resolution

§1. Introduction

168. In the previous chapter, our examination of sports governance offered a useful backdrop for the general approach taken by sport governing bodies in Trinidad and Tobago to the resolution of disputes. Various constitutions displayed a spectrum of clauses that ranged from simplistic and outdated to complex and sophisticated.

169. A related question, however, is whether disputes which emanate from the decisions of NGBs can be challenged by way of judicial review, given what is often described as a quasi-public law function performed by sports governing bodies.

§2. Judicial Review in Trinidad and Tobago Sport

170. The Judicial Review Act Chapter 7:08 offers early clarity with regard to the intended scope of the Act. It states in section 5 that an 'application for judicial review of a decision of an inferior Court, tribunal, public body, public authority or a person acting in the exercise of a public duty or function in accordance with any law shall be made to the Court in accordance with this Act and in such manner as may be prescribed by Rules of Court'.

171. This is an interesting statutory provision in the context of sport as it refers to a 'public body', a 'public authority' or 'a person acting in the exercise of a public duty or function in accordance with any law'. It is the term 'public body' that poses the most legal difficulties in Trinidad and Tobago due to the partial proclamation of the 2015 Public Procurement and Disposal of Public Property Act (The Public Procurement Act)[107] In the Public Procurement Act, a 'public body' includes, *inter alia*:

(1) a State-controlled enterprise;
(2) a Ministry or a department or division of a Ministry;
(3) a statutory body responsibility for which is assigned to a Minister of Government;
(4) a body corporate or unincorporated entity in relation to any function which it exercises on behalf of the State;
(5) a body corporate or unincorporated entity in relation to any function, project, scheme or arrangement which involves the use by it, of public money.[108]

172. 'Public money' is itself defined to include money which is received or receivable by a public body or which is spent or committed for future expenditure

107. Act No. 1 of 2015.
108. Section 4.

by a public body.[109] Since a public body includes a Government ministry, it means that the MSYA in Trinidad and Tobago is a public body as is the Ministry of Finance. Almost all NGBs in Trinidad and Tobago receive money from either of these two ministries in the form of grants or subventions. It means, then, that according to the Public Procurement Act, any NGB that receives money from the Government through its representative ministry is also a public body.

173. Returning to section 5 of the Judicial Review Act, decisions of a public body are subject to judicial review via the applicable procedure. Read together with the Public Procurement Act, an eye-opening consequence results, namely, that sports governing bodies in Trinidad and Tobago which receive state funding are amenable to judicial review. It is unlikely that the Members of Parliament or the legislative drafters intended to capture sports governing bodies in the net of entities subject to judicial review but, as currently drafted, this is the effect of the relevant statutory provisions.

174. Furthermore, the above-mentioned Boxing Board has a somewhat unique construct since its members are appointed by the Minister of Sport pursuant to the Boxing Control Act. This places the Boxing Board within more than one of the definitions of a 'public body' in the Public Procurement Act as it could possibly be deemed a state-controlled enterprise or a statutory body responsibility for which is assigned to a Minister of Government. Even if doubt existed about the applicability of those two definitions, the Boxing Board also receives Government funding thus making it an entity that receives 'public money'.

I. The General Rule

175. The oft-cited sections of the decision in *R v. Disciplinary Committee of the Jockey Club ex parte Aga Khan*[110] are a useful starting point for any discussion of judicial review in sport. In *Mullins v. The Appeal Board of the Jockey Club*[111] the head note in *Aga Khan* was cited as a way of summarising the general principle:

> Although the Jockey Club exercised dominant control over racing activities in Great Britain its powers and duties were in no sense governmental but derived from the contractual relationship between the club and those agreeing to be bound by the Rules of Racing; that such powers gave rise to private rights enforceable by private action in which effective relief by way of declaration, injunction and damages was available; and that, accordingly, the club's decision was not amenable to judicial review.

109. *Ibid.*
110. [1993] 1 WLR 909.
111. [2005]EWHC 2197.

176. The court in *Mullins* expounded on this general rule by noting that the test applied by the Court of Appeal in *Aga Khan* was whether the powers and duties of the Jockey Club were governmental.[112] The Court addressed this issue by noting the following dictum of the Master of the Rolls in *Aga Khan*:

> I have little hesitation in accepting the applicant's contention that the Jockey Club effectively regulates a significant national activity, exercising powers which affect the public and are exercised in the interest of the public. I am willing to accept that if the Jockey Club did not regulate this activity the government would probably be driven to create a public body to do so. But the Jockey Club is not in its origin, its history, its constitution or (least of all) its membership a public body.

177. This is a crucial observation that is worth further consideration especially in view of the nuances of sports governance in Trinidad and Tobago. The Master of the Rolls identified a few essential features of the operations of the Jockey Club:

(1) it regulated a significant national activity;
(2) it exercised powers which affected the public; and
(3) its exercise of powers was done in the interest of the public.

178. Yet, these actions were qualified by looking at the context of the Jockey Club's existence in which it was observed that the Jockey Club was *not* a public body in four areas:

(1) its origin;
(2) its history;
(3) its constitution; and
(4) its membership.

The *Aga Khan* criteria are a helpful reference point.

II. Regulation of a Significant National Activity

179. In Aga Khan, no definition was offered to assist in determining the meaning of a 'significant national activity'. It is uncertain, then, whether it referred to the popularity of the sport, its general prominence within society or some other description. Perhaps if legislation such as the National Sports Act of Canada[113] existed in

112. *Ibid.*, at para. 22.
113. S.C. 1994, c. 16.

many countries across the globe, this question would be less speculative. That Canadian statute names hockey and lacrosse as the national sports of Canada, with ice hockey being declared the national winter sport and lacrosse as the national summer sport.[114]

180. In Canada, then, it would appear safe to say that the respective governing bodies for ice hockey and lacrosse regulate a significant national activity. The position is not as watertight when one considers the practice of popular sports in Trinidad and Tobago such as football, cricket, athletics, basketball and swimming. There is simply insufficient empirical data to gauge the 'significance' of a sport.

III. Exercising Powers Which Affect the Public or Are in the Public Interest

181. Again, in the absence of a definition of the expression 'which affects the public' one runs the risk of being, at best, subjective in one's analysis of a sport's national impact. One step in the direction of definitional clarity occurred in the 2016 case *of Thema Yakaena Williams v. Trinidad and Tobago Gymnastics Federation, Marquez, Wattley, Lue Shue & Lue Shue*[115] which centred on a selection dispute in the lead up to the 2016 Rio Summer Olympics.

182. A preliminary issue about the validity and applicability of an arbitration clause was ventilated before Justice Frank Seepersad. Seepersad J. held the view that the matters before him were of national importance, noting further that there was, in his words, 'a very evident public interest concern in this matter and the selection process for representation at the Olympics is an issue that extends beyond the insular concerns of the parties to this matter and is one in which every citizen has a vested interest'.[116]

183. For Seepersad J. the matter became one of national importance and constituted a public interest concern because it involved representation at the highest level of global sport, the Olympics. The context of the case made it even more outstanding since it was the first time that Trinidad and Tobago would be sending a gymnast to the Olympic Games. Here, both history and the magnitude of the event contributed to the conclusion that the issues at hand were public interest matters.

184. The natural follow-up question, then, would be whether the Claimant's challenge in *Williams v. TTGF* could be founded on judicial review grounds. Although this issue was not raised as part of the relief sought in the substantive claim, it was instructive to note the court's statements in its November 2018 ruling as it addressed the duty of fairness and the opportunity to be heard. The court noted

114. *Ibid.*, at s. 2.
115. Claim CV 2016-02608.
116. *Ibid.*, at para. 22.

that in 'matters of public law, a public body, even where there is owed a duty of fairness to an individual, may relax the observance of those rules'.[117]

185. The discussion on public law, to some degree, almost came out of nowhere as it was not a matter under consideration. It left the impression that, in the court's view, the Trinidad and Tobago Gymnastics Federation (TTGF) was, in fact, a public body subject to public law remedies. There could be no other logical reason for the court to embark on a distillation of the powers of public authorities in the context of the duty of fairness, if the principles it espoused were not intended to apply to the TTGF. Perhaps this was a missed opportunity for the local courts to add legal clarity on the amenability of sporting bodies to judicial review.

186. Similarly, on 17 December 2018 the court in *Dinanath Ramnarine and others v. Trinidad and Tobago Cricket Board*,[118] while focusing on the main issue as to whether outgoing Executive Committee members should be eligible to vote at annual general meetings of the TTCB, also made passing mention of the judicial review question. In fact, it was the Claimants who sought leave to apply for judicial review, which application was actually dismissed.

187. The notable observation, though, is that the court failed to address whether judicial review was the appropriate form of redress to be sought by the Claimants. The only comment on judicial review came in the concluding paragraphs as follows:

> As discussed above, it is for TTCB to decide what rules it considers to be in the best interests of its members and the sport in general. There is nothing to suggest that the rules are inherently unfair or deviate from established principles of democracy or public policy. I would go further to say that, had the Claimants' application for leave to apply for judicial review not been combined with the substantive hearing, leave would not have been granted as the Claimants have not met the threshold requirements of demonstrating that they have an arguable case with a realistic prospect of success.
>
> The following passage from the decision of Thakur J. of the Supreme Court of India, Civil Appellate Jurisdiction, in *Board of Cricket Control in India v. Cricket Association of Bihar & Ors. Civ App. No 4235 of 2014* at paragraph 93, provides an appropriate conclusion:
>
> > *'In K Murugon v Fencing Association of India, Jabalpur and ors (1991) 2 SCC 412 this Court held that sports in India have assumed great importance for the community while international sports have assumed greater importance over the past few decades. Despite this, however, several sports bodies in this country have got involved in group fights leading to litigation in the process losing sight of the objectives which such societies and bodies are meant to achieve. This Court therefore emphasized the need for setting right the working of societies rather than adjudicating*

---

117. *Ibid.*, at para. 86.
118. Claim No. CV 2016-03556.

upon the individual's right to office by reference to provisions of law relating to meetings (and) injunctions ...'
For the reasons given above, the Claimants' application for judicial review is hereby dismissed.[119] [Emphasis original]

188. In citing the *Bihar* decision from India, the local court seemed to be asserting that it was not appropriate for the courts to get involved in the electoral disputes of autonomous sporting bodies, although there would be a greater willingness to intervene with respect to the broader issue of whether governing bodies were effective in the management of their respective sports. Yet, the fact that the court chose to cite this case may have offered insight into its view of the TTCB's role.

189. The court in *Bihar* was quite forceful in its view of the nature of the functions of the Board of Control for Cricket in India (BCCI). It stated, *inter alia*:

> Any organization or entity that has such pervasive control over the game and its affairs and such powers as can make dreams end up in smoke or come true cannot be said to be undertaking any private activity. The functions of the Board are clearly public functions, which, till such time the State intervenes to takeover the same, remain in the nature of public functions, no matter discharged by a society registered under the Registration of Societies Act. Suffice it to say that if the Government not only allows an autonomous/private body to discharge functions which it could in law takeover or regulate but even lends its assistance to such a non-government body to undertake such functions which by their very nature are public functions, it cannot be said that the functions are not public functions or that the entity discharging the same is not answerable on the standards generally applicable to judicial review of State action.[120]

190. On the question of judicial review, it is submitted that the court in *Ramnarine v. TTCB* could have expanded its discussion of the *Bihar* decision, rather than simply quoting from it in the conclusion. It seemed to have accepted the application for judicial review from the Claimants, although it was ultimately dismissed. Yet, the dismissal was not based on there being a pursuit of an incorrect legal remedy but instead on a failure to meet the threshold of likelihood of success.

191. As was the case in the aforementioned substantive *Thema Williams* ruling, the court in *Ramnarine* appears to have assumed that judicial review applied to the decisions of the respective NGBs. It is hoped that in the near future the courts in Trinidad and Tobago would address this question head on, or at the very least, justify its acceptance of judicial review applications in the context of sporting bodies.

119. *Ibid.*, at paras 41–43.
120. Board of Control for Cricket in *India v. Cricket Association of Bihar* and Ors, Civil Appeal No. 4235 of 2014, at para. 30.

IV. Public or Private Bodies?

192. The decision in *R. v. The Football Association Limited ex parte The Football League Limited*[121] was cited in *Aga Khan* and also provided legal guidance of the applicability of judicial review. In ex parte *Football League*, Rose J. had to consider whether the Football Association was susceptible to judicial review. He noted:

> I have crossed a great deal of ground in order to reach what, on the authorities, is the clear and inescapable conclusion for me that the FA is not a body susceptible to judicial review either in general or, more particularly, at the instigation of the League with whom it is contractually bound. Despite its virtually monopolistic powers and the importance of its decisions to many members of the public who are not contractually bound to it, it is, in my judgment, a domestic body whose powers arise from and duties exist in private law only. I find no sign of underpinning directly or indirectly by any organ or agency of the State or any potential government interest, as Simon Brown J. put it in *Wachmann*, nor is there any evidence to suggest that if the FA did not exist the State would intervene to create a public body to perform its functions. On the contrary, the evidence of commercial interest in the professional game is such as to suggest that a far more likely intervener to run football would be a television or similar company rooted in the entertainment business or a commercial company seeking advertising benefits such as presently provides sponsorship in one form or another.

193. Rose J.'s analysis mirrors that in *Aga Khan*. In assessing the operations of the Football Association (F.A.) as a governing body, he noted that:

(1) it had monopolistic powers; and
(2) its decisions were important to many members of the public.

194. Yet, he was equally lucid in stating that the F.A.'s powers arose from private law and that its duties also existed in private law.

195. There has been general agreement with the *Aga Khan* philosophy in legal circles. The difficulty for Trinidad and Tobago will be reconciling the prevailing case law with the provisions of the Judicial Review Act and the Public Procurement Act when read together and applied to the sporting context. This juxtaposition is yet to be tested.

121. [1993] 2 All ER 833.

§3. Disciplinary Proceedings

196. Many of the legal controversies in the Trinidad and Tobago sports sector have arisen out of attempts by NGBs to discipline members under their jurisdiction. The challenge is often two-fold:

(1) the constitutions of the NGBs fail to include properly drafted clauses on disciplinary proceedings or omit them altogether; and
(2) the disciplinary and/or appeals committees lack independence and impartiality since oftentimes, members of the Executive Committee of the respective NGBs sit on the various adjudicatory panels.

197. In this regard, the previously mentioned 2018 constitutional template of Cricket Trinidad and Tobago (CT&T) as well as the 2015 revised constitution of the TTFA provide sound models.

198. Article 28.07 of the 2018 CT&T constitutional template provides for a Tribunal which sits as an appellate body of final instance and which has the power to agree or disagree with decisions made by the respective disciplinary committees below it. It can reduce or increase penalties, or it can refer matters back to the tribunals below for re-hearing. This proposed structure provides much-needed clarity in the system.

199. Section H of the 2015 TTFA constitution provides clear stipulations of how the various judicial bodies will function. Articles 60–67 deal respectively with the following topics:

- Judicial bodies (Article 60)
- The Disciplinary Committee (Article 61)
- The Ethics Committee (Article 62)
- The Appeal Committee (Article 63)
- Disciplinary Measures (Article 64)
- Arbitration (Article 65)
- Jurisdiction (Article 66)
- The Court of Arbitration for Sport (CAS).

200. Built in to these provisions are clear procedural steps that allow for certainty and predictability in the disciplinary process. The content of Article 66 is fairly rare in NGB constitutions in Trinidad and Tobago and is a commendable inclusion as it specifies the boundary lines of the TTFA's jurisdiction (internal national disputes) as compared to FIFA's (international disputes).

201. The absence of these elements has led to various challenges to the decisions of NGBs in Trinidad and Tobago, including within the sport of badminton. In

Nekeisha Blake v. Trinidad and Tobago Badminton Association,[122] the Appellant badminton player, Ms. Nekeisha Blake appealed against the decision of the Disciplinary Committee of the Trinidad and Tobago Badminton Association (The Badminton Association) to exclude her indefinitely from the sport. The matters to be determined by the Appeals Committee were as follows:

(1) Did the Disciplinary Committee in hearing the Blake matter commit alleged breaches of procedure that ran contrary to the principles of natural justice?
(2) If the procedure adopted was not deemed to be in violation of the principles of natural justice, is the life ban proportionate with the gravity of the alleged breaches?
(3) If not, should there be a reduction in or complete elimination of the current life ban?[123]

202. The Appeals Committee found that the lifetime ban imposed by the Badminton Association was a disproportionate one and that the principles of natural justice had also been breached by the Disciplinary Committee. However, it also found that the Appellant sought to frustrate the disciplinary process by her failure to attend the hearings and her decision to make disparaging remarks about the Badminton Association on national media.

203. In substituting a one-year ban for the lifetime ban, the Appeals Committee recommended, usefully, that Badminton Association "constitute a special subcommittee *to develop detailed rules to govern discipline of members.* This should include guidelines for (i) preferring of charges (ii) notification to members and (iii) listing the procedure guiding hearings and decision making. *Such a protocol will ensure certainty* and minimi[ze] breaches of Natural Justice and Allegations relative to same'.[124] [Emphasis added] The need for clear rules, procedural precision and legal certainty emerged in the *Nekeisha Blake* decision and must be flagged by NGBs as specific targets to be pursued and attained.

204. In *Creed v. Central Audit Committee*,[125] Dean-Armorer J. reiterated the primacy of natural justice principles when she ruled that the Claimants, which included a former Permanent Secretary in the Ministry of Sport in Trinidad and Tobago, had not been treated fairly by the Central Audit Committee (CAC)[126] when they were not afforded a proper opportunity to be heard and to make representations. This breach of procedural fairness occurred against the backdrop of the allegations made against the Claimants that their oversight of and/or involvement in the controversial

122. Decision of the Appeals Committee of the Trinidad and Tobago Badminton Association (undated).
123. *Ibid.*, at para. 18.
124. *Ibid.*, post-para. 46, at p. 14.
125. *Ashwin Creed et al v. Central Audit Committee* [TT 2016 HC] 230.
126. The Central Audit Committee acted under the instructions of the Minister of Finance.

Lifesport Programme[127] revealed improper conduct, including poor financial management and breaches of procurement practices. The Court also found that the conduct of the CAC in acting unfairly frustrated the legitimate expectation of the Claimants.

§4. ADR: The Growth of Sports Mediation and Arbitration

205. The phenomenal evolution of the CAS over the past three decades as a competent tribunal for the resolution of sports-related disputes has shone a positive spotlight on mediation and arbitration.[128] Sometimes seen as a well-kept secret, mediation continues to blossom quietly in sporting circles, with there being an increasing willingness to include mediation as a pre-arbitration step in dispute resolution clauses of sports governing bodies.

206. By way of example, the Kokaram Report mentioned in the previous chapter proposes in an appendix the Draft Mediation Rules of the CT&T Cricket Mediation Council.[129] Article 2.01 defines mediation as 'a non-binding and informal procedure in which each party undertakes to attempt in good faith to negotiate with the other party with a view to settling their dispute'. Article 2.02 expands on the definition by outlining the scope of the mediation. It states:

> 'Disputes also include any matter in which the parties are engaged in litigation. Mediation is also provided for the resolution of contractual disputes. Disputes related to disciplinary matters such as doping issues, match-fixing and corruption are excluded from mediation. However, where the circumstances so require and the parties expressly agree, disputes related to disciplinary matters may be submitted to mediation.

207. The proposed exclusion of certain types of disputes from mediation, especially those of a disciplinary nature accords with mediation best practice.

208. Arbitration is a creature of contract. Defined by Moses as a private system of adjudication[130] it has also been called a 'growth industry[131]'. Paulsson's viewpoint is instructive:

---

127. The Lifesport Programme was an initiative of the Ministry of Sport to use the avenue of sport to provide positive alternative lifestyles to 'at risk' youths in the country.
128. This section of the chapter is an expanded and amended version of an article originally published in the September 2014 Volume of the *Global Sports Law and Taxation Reports*.
129. Appendix 5.
130. Margaret L. Moses, *The Principles and Practice of International Commercial Arbitration* 1 (Cambridge University Press 2d ed. 2012).
131. James A.R. Nafziger, *Arbitration of Rights and Obligations in the International Sports Arena*, 35 Val. U. L. Rev. 357 (2001).

> There is however a more credible line of reasoning in support of exclusive extrajudicial authority to settle sports disputes. This is the concept that the exclusive disciplinary jurisdiction of sports officials has been granted by the parties to the dispute on a consensual basis; the ordinary courts are thus ousted by virtue of the familiar contractual mechanisms of prorogation.[132]

209. His allusion to the consensual basis upon which sports arbitral tribunals have been given exclusive dispute resolution jurisdiction reflects both the fact and the fiction of the process. Fact: because judicial intervention is generally discouraged and sporting federations' autonomy encouraged. Fiction: because the threat of exclusion from sport's mega events militates against true and genuine consent to arbitration by athletes.

210. The issue of consent apart, current trends in international arbitration suggest that the question of setting aside an arbitrator's award is gaining prominence and giving rise to new jurisprudential developments both inside and outside of the sports arena. The March 2014 judgment of High Court Judge Andre Des Vignes in Trinidad and Tobago is a case in point and will receive due consideration below.

211. Mc Ardle has noted that arbitration 'offers the potential for disputes to be resolved on the basis of universally acknowledged principles, specifically accepted by the parties and not limited by the vagaries of national legal systems. They are binding, recognised by national legal systems and can be enforced under national laws should such an eventuality arise'. He adds that as 'with other structures of arbitration, the work of CAS and other sports-specific systems would be rendered untenable if the national legal systems did not recognise their validity and were unable to enforce them, so the willingness of national courts to do so is a pre-requisite'.[133] These are critical elements of sports arbitration since the ability to enforce arbitral awards as High Court judgments lends credibility to the system and offers comfort to the disputants. At the same time, this perhaps is also the weakness of sports mediation, since its legally binding effect is only activated if there has been a settlement agreement between the parties.

212. Sher has made the salient observation that the 'new regime for domestic commercial arbitration reflects how far Australia has come in creating a substantively distinct jurisdiction for commercial dispute resolution as an alternative to the courts. An avowed desire to avoid the replication of processes through the courts motivated the authors of the UNCITRAL Model Law on International Commercial

132. Jan Paulsson, *Arbitration of International Sports Disputes, The Court of Arbitration for Sport 1984-2004*' 41 (I.S. Blackshaw, R.C.R. Siekmann & J.W. Soek, eds., TMC Asser Press 2006).
133. David Mc Ardle, *Dispute Resolution in Sport, Athletes, Law and Arbitration* 26 (Routledge 2015).

Arbitration (the Model Law). Their aim was to restrict drastically the scope for curial intervention in order to achieve speedy, cost-effective, fair and final resolution of disputes'.[134]

213. The four goals articulated above mirror the objectives of most, if not all, organisations involved in ADR. Predictably, each target is experiencing its own level of success, with speed and cost varying from country to country and industry to industry.

214. As far as fairness is concerned, sport arbitrations underwent some scrutiny with the 1992 *Elmar Gundel*[135] challenge. Arising from that case the ICAS was born, with a view to producing clearer separation 'organisationally and financially'[136] between the IOC and the CAS, a body conceived by the IOC about thirty-five years ago. The Swiss Federal Tribunal in *Gundel* endorsed 'not without hesitation',[137] the impartiality of the CAS, cautioning that an 'arbitral tribunal which is an organ of an association appearing as a party to the dispute does not ensure a sufficient degree of independence'.[138]

215. The fourth objective, the finality of arbitration, is the focus of this section of the chapter.

I. Setting aside the Arbitration Award

216. In another round of battles between the governing body of Caribbean cricket, CWI,[139] and the players' union, the 'the WIPA', the full cycle of dispute resolution was unveiled. By July 2010, negotiations and mediation led to no breakthrough, thus leading to the arbitral process pursuant to the Arbitration Act Chapter 5:01 of Trinidad and Tobago ('the TT Arbitration Act') under the jurisdiction of a sole panellist, Seenath Jairam, S.C.

217. The arbitration clause usually inserted into the Collective Bargaining Agreement (CBA) between these two parties stated as follows: 'If there is no resolution of the grievance by mediation, the aggrieved party may refer the matter to an arbitration tribunal for the expressed purpose of hearing the grievance and determining the matter.' Arbitrator Jairam made his award on 7 December 2011('the Jairam Award') ordering that CWI pay over USD 1 million representing loss of

134. Julian Sher, *When Even Fraud is Not Nearly Enough. Recourse Against Arbitral Awards and Public Policy Considerations: An Anglo-Australian Perspective*, 80 *Int. J. Arbitration, Med. Dispute Manage.* (April 2014).
135. *Gundel v. International Equestrian Federation* (FEI).
136. Matthieu Reeb, CAS Secretary General, as quoted in *Sport, Mediation and Arbitration*, Prof Dr Ian Blackshaw 152 (T.M.C. Asser Press 2009).
137. Paulsson, *supra*, n. 132 at 47.
138. *Ibid.*, at p. 45.
139. Formerly known as the WICB.

earnings, loss of sponsorship opportunity, gate receipts, mediation and arbitration costs, legal fees, interest, and nominal damages.

218. CWI applied to the High Court citing eight grounds upon which the award should be set aside or remitted to the arbitrator pursuant to sections 18 and 19 of the TT Arbitration Act. Des Vignes J. set aside the arbitrator's award, a decision which was subsequently appealed by the WIPA.

II. The Rationale for Setting aside the Jairam Award

219. At the heart of the order to set aside the Jairam Award were the errors of law identified by Justice Des Vignes. The possibility of setting aside was contemplated by the parties in the drafting of the CBA. Yet, this preliminary point still had to be ventilated as the WIPA questioned whether the court had the jurisdiction to determine the matter. The resolution would come by construing Article XI 4(b) of the CBA, which stated that except 'on a point of law, the decision of the arbitration tribunal shall be final and binding on both parties'.

220. The judge expeditiously disposed of the issue noting that the language of the Article was clear and unambiguous[140] and that 'provided that the issues raised by the WICB concern the Arbitrator's interpretation of points of law, this court is sufficiently vested with authority to review the decision of the Arbitrator'.[141]

221. It is in this regard that recent developments in Australia and England, in particular, are worthy of mention. Lord Steyn in *Lesotho Highlands v. Impregilo*[142] alluded to the 'right of appeal "on a question of law"'[143] as articulated in section 69 of the United Kingdom (UK) 1996 Arbitration Act, the question of law referring specifically to 'a question of the law of England' as defined in section 82(1) of the 1996 Act.

222. Sher noted, though, that traditionally it has been a feature of English arbitration to restrict judicial intervention.[144] He added that by 'enacting the Arbitration Act 1996 (the English Arbitration Act), the UK Parliament adopted the Model Law, but went much further, by severely restricting the possibility of setting aside in particular'.[145] This approach, he observed, confirms the practice of the English courts to confine 'setting aside to only the most egregious and reprehensible of cases'.[146]

140. CV 2012-00046-WICB v. WIPA, Des Vignes J. at para. 39.
141. *Ibid.*
142. [2005] 3 All E.R. 789.
143. *Ibid.*, at para. 3.
144. Sher, *supra*, n. 134.
145. *Ibid.*
146. *Ibid.*

223. The position in England, then, is that arbitral awards will be respected as final and binding, with setting aside occurring only in the most extreme circumstances.

224. Further, Sher has contrasted the Australian statutory ethos, stating that, if the making of an arbitral award was contrary to public policy, it could trigger recourse against the award, including setting aside.[147] Within the last decade, Commercial Arbitration Acts have been enacted in Australia at the State level, complementing the adoption of the International Arbitration Act into Federal law.

225. A useful question has consequently been asked in the Australian context: 'What is the test for remittal rather than setting aside?'[148] This query is apposite in the Trinidad and Tobago setting as well, in the light of the court's response to the Jairam Award. Justice Des Vignes was satisfied that errors of law warranted a setting aside and not an 'order for remission'.[149] An Australian judge would probably concur, with his English counterpart likely to dissent.

226. Notably, both England and Australia currently have access to the expertise of sports-specific dispute resolution bodies, respectively, Sport Resolutions UK and the Oceania Registry of the CAS. In a recent case emanating from the CAS Sydney Registry, the sole arbitrator made the significant point that he 'would arbitrate on the dispute and render an Award in conformity with the agreement between the parties to submit their dispute for arbitration before the CAS'[150] It appears, then, that his safeguard from having a challenge lodged against his award would be to comply with the terms of the arbitration agreement. In any event, appeals against CAS awards are rare and typically restricted to very limited grounds.

227. It is conceivable that the Des Vignes ruling could be a catalyst in shaping sports-related arbitration law in Trinidad and Tobago and, perhaps, even the wider Caribbean. Yet, the decision may also have indirectly endorsed the wisdom of the well-established practice of using subject matter experts in ADR generally.

228. This analysis is offered in view of the fact that, although arbitrator Jairam identified the relevant principles of contract interpretation, the judge's appraisal was that Jairam 'failed to apply these principles'.[151] Des Vignes J. added that the Arbitrator's construction of the CBA flouted business common sense.[152]

229. The latter observation is reminiscent of Lord Mustill's message in the *The Chrysalis*,[153] a message which Tweeddale succinctly summarised when noting that

147. *Ibid.*
148. *Ibid.*
149. Des Vignes J, *supra*, at para. 108.
150. *Australia Sports Anti-Doping Agency v. Bannister* Ref. A 1/2013 at para. 18.
151. Des Vignes J, *supra*, at paras 72 and 76.
152. *Ibid.*
153. [1983] 2 All E.R 658.

Mustill J. 'recognised that a court might be less willing to substitute its own judgment for that of the arbitrator if the issue concerned an area of industry in which the arbitrator had extensive practical experience'.[154]

230. Where the CAS excels, the Trinidad and Tobago and, by extension, the Caribbean sports ADR mechanism, underachieves. The reality is that there is a dearth of arbitrators in the region with a strong history of practical experience in sports-related disputes, thus putting the Jairam Award into some context. The judge's comment that the arbitrator's decision flouted business common sense was not an indictment on his competence but rather may have reflected a possible lack of familiarity with the overlap between the commercialisation and juridification of international cricket in the twenty-first century.

231. Conversely, arbitrator Ian Mill, Q.C., although not from the Caribbean, had a different narrative.

III. The Ian Mill Arbitral Award: FIFA World Cup 2006

232. Although previous academic consideration has been given to this case,[155] the current discussion explores a few additional areas, including the governing arbitration law and procedure as well as the binding nature of an arbitration award.

233. The litigants were both from Trinidad and Tobago, the Claimants being sixteen football players who represented the country at the FIFA 2006 World Cup in Germany, while the Defendants were the NGB for football, the TTFA (then known as the TTFF) and its former president, the late Oliver Camps.

234. The relevant arbitration provision, Clause 14, was found in the Player Agreements which were executed before the World Cup. It stated as follows:

> Disputes/Arbitration
> The parties shall submit all disputes arising out of or relating to this Agreement before an arbitration panel or a mediator appointed by the TTFF in Trinidad and Tobago … The award shall be rendered in such form that a judgment may be entered thereon. An appeal arising out of a decision of the arbitration or mediation shall be to an appeal committee appointed by CONCACAF and any appeal therefrom shall be to the Court of Arbitration for Sport, LAUSANNE, Switzerland.[156]

154. Andrew Tweeddale et al., *Section 69 of the English Arbitration Act 1996-When Fact and Law Collide*, 80 *Int. J. Arbitration, Med. Dispute Manage*, 139 (April 2014).
155. 'ADR in Caribbean Sport'-*Global Sports Law and Taxation Reports*, June 2011, J. Tyrone Marcus.
156. CV 2007-02238-*Andrews et al. v. TTFF and Camps-Rampersad J* at p. 3.

235. The procedural direction of this dispute was somewhat unorthodox and potentially confusing. The case started as a High Court breach of contract claim by the players, alleging non-payment of money due and owing to them arising from their participation in the 2006 World Cup. An initial question that arose was whether, according to Clause 14 of the Player Agreement, the first course of action was to the High Court. The wording of the clause suggests that the dispute should have gone to either arbitration or mediation in Trinidad and Tobago.

236. On the facts of the case, arbitration did take place but only after the High Court claim was filed. The way that the arbitral process was engaged is noteworthy, since it was the Defendants who applied for a stay of proceedings pursuant to section 7 of the TT Arbitration Act Chapter 5:01.

237. The matter is further complicated given the signing of a new Arbitration Agreement in September 2007 ('the September Agreement') which provided for arbitration under the English Arbitration Act 1996 and not the TT Arbitration Act. With the inherent confidentiality of arbitration proceedings, understandably, crucial documents have not come into the public domain. One can only speculate that the new Arbitration Agreement superseded Clause 14, which clause, in arbitration law and practice, is sufficient in and of itself to constitute an arbitration agreement.

238. The arbitral award was made by Ian Mill Q.C. ('the Mill Award'), on behalf of the Sports Dispute Resolution Panel under whose auspices the English arbitration took place. The Defendants expressed concerns after sections of the award were leaked to the media and decided to re-engage the High Court. If Clause 14 still applied, it is reasonable to assume that their next step could have been to a CONCACAF[157] Appeal Committee.

239. Clause 10 of the September Agreement now becomes instructive. It said: 'The Arbitration award shall be final and binding on the parties and shall be registered as a judgment of the High Court of Trinidad and Tobago in these proceedings and enforceable accordingly, provided however that either party shall have a right of appeal to the Court of Arbitration for Sport but only with leave of the Arbitrator'.[158] This clause left available a right of appeal to CAS, an option which evidently was not explored.

240. The entire process suggests, at least, two possibilities: a failure to adhere to procedural guidelines or in-built flexibility which is a hallmark of ADR processes. The question still begs, though, whether the CAS would have been a more appropriate forum for this matter to be heard with regard to the Defendants' challenge to the SDRP arbitration. In fact, it is also important to consider whether the stay of proceedings did contemplate the exhaustion of the entire arbitral process including an

---

157. Confederation of North, Central American and Caribbean Association Football.
158. Rampersad J, *supra*, n. 156 at 13.

appeal to CAS. It may be that, since the Defendants sought to challenge the validity of the agreement itself and not the actual arbitral award, they returned to the High Court as against approaching CAS.

241. To the chagrin of Trinidad and Tobago nationals, this case endured an eight-year legal roller coaster and, although the approach to the SDRP with a right of appeal to CAS was a commendable measure, since it placed the imbroglio before two specialist sports disputes tribunals, it is hard not to conclude that an opportunity for earlier resolution was missed.

IV. Setting aside the Arbitration Agreement

242. Very early in his judgment, Rampersad J. summarised the key areas for determination, stating that the case 'specifically examines the question of breach of confidence in arbitration. Incidental to this principle of confidentiality is the issue of the binding nature of the arbitration award and its enforcement in the High Court of Trinidad and Tobago'.[159] However, the twist in this case, as mentioned earlier, was the Defendants' attempt to invalidate the September Agreement and not the Mill Award.

243. Justice Rampersad further distilled the issues down to one, namely, 'whether the disclosure of the award was a fundamental breach of the terms of the arbitration agreement such that the agreement ought reasonably to have been set aside'. [Emphasis original]. He did not have much difficulty in finding, in light of the prevailing law, that the confidentiality obligation, so fundamental to the arbitral process, was breached by the Claimants. The SDRP Rules also expressly provided for the confidentiality of the proceedings. The salient question that followed was whether that breach went to the root of the contract leading to a repudiation of the entire agreement.[160] Justice Rampersad answered in the negative.

244. Citing Redfern and Hunter in the Law and Practice of Commercial Arbitration, the judge noted that there 'are limits to the confidentiality of the arbitral process ... for example ... the existence (and perhaps the contents) of an award may become public knowledge if the winning party is obliged to take action in the courts to enforce it'.[161] He concluded that the arbitration agreement remained irrevocable in accordance with section 3 of the TT Arbitration Act. Additionally, pursuant to the 1958 New York Convention[162] and section 6 of the Arbitration (Foreign Arbitral Awards) Act Chapter 5:30 of Trinidad and Tobago, the court granted leave for the Mill Award to be registered and enforced as a judgment of the High Court of Trinidad and Tobago.

159. *Ibid.*, at pp. 3–4.
160. *Ibid.*, at 10.
161. *Ibid.*, at 12.
162. The United Nations Convention on the Recognition and Enforcement of Foreign Arbitral Awards (New York, 10 Jun. 1958).

V. The Thema Williams Decision: Rio 2016 Olympic Selection Dispute

245. On 26 November 2018 Justice Frank Seepersad issued one of the most significant sporting decisions in Trinidad and Tobago's history. Following his aforementioned April 2017 ruling on a preliminary matter concerning an application for a stay of High Court proceedings for the purpose of arbitration, he proceeded to rule on the substantive claim. The judgment offered an opportune and useful disposition on the law of agency, administrative law, implied terms in contract law, the tort of unlawful means conspiracy, procuring a breach of contract and the law of remedies, all in the context of an Olympic selection dispute.

246. At the heart of the dispute was the sudden substitution of the Claimant Thema Williams by the First Defendant, the TTGF. Williams was replaced by the alternate athlete, Marisa Dick, after the former's coach suggested in an email that the injury she was carrying placed doubt on her ability to give her best performance at the Olympic Test Event being held in Rio de Janeiro, Brazil, a few months before the 2016 Summer Olympics in that same city.

247. Five main legal issues arose for the court's determination:

(1) whether the TTGF breached its contractual obligations with Williams under their selection process and the athlete's agreement executed between Williams and the TTGF. These contractual obligations were to treat her fairly, in good faith and with a duty of fidelity;
(2) whether the TTGF was in breach of its duty towards Williams by taking a decision to replace her as the selected athlete without giving her or her representatives an opportunity to be heard or to make representations;
(3) whether the second to fifth defendants, who were all members of the TTGF's Executive Committee, individually owed a fiduciary duty to Williams and further breached that duty;
(4) whether the second to fifth defendants were individually liable for procuring a breach of the athlete's agreement and, further, whether they acted with a common design to withdraw Williams and replace her with Marisa Dick; and
(5) whether the second to fifth defendants engaged in an unlawful means conspiracy to replace Williams which conduct should render them personally liable to her for damages.[163]

248. A brief overview of the court's disposition of each of these issues follows below.

163. *Thema Yakaena Williams v. Trinidad and Tobago Gymnastics Federation et al*-CV 2016-02608, para. 13.

A. Breach of Contract and Opportunity to Be Heard

249. There was no disagreement in this case that a contract existed between the TTGF and Williams. In fact, it was Williams' pleaded case that the express contractual terms could be found cumulatively in the athlete's agreement and the selection process.[164] However, Williams urged the court to imply a term into the contract, namely that the TTGF could not substitute her without first giving her, her coach or her medical personnel an opportunity to be heard and to make representations.[165]

250. On this issue, the court concluded that there was no merit in Williams' contention that she or her medical personnel should have been consulted by virtue of any implied term either in the athlete's agreement or in the selection process.[166] Seepersad J. noted the following:

> It is settled law that the Courts are not permitted to re-write the contract or to read words into contractual provisions which contradic[t] its express terms or the parties' intention. In the case of *Attorney General of Belize & Ors v Belize Telecom Ltd & Anor [2009] UKPC 10*, Lord Hoffman at paragraph 16 said: '*The Court has no power to improve upon the instrument which it is called upon to construe, whether it be a contract, a statute or articles of association. It cannot introduce terms to make it fairer or more reasonable. It is concerned only to discover what the instrument means.*' [Emphasis original]

251. The court in *Williams* was clear in its finding that the Claimant did not meet the legal standard required for any term to be implied. Seepersad J., in so ruling, cited the five necessary conditions for a contractual term to be implied, as outlined in *BP Refinery v. Shire of Hastings,*[167] namely:

(1) it must be reasonable and equitable;
(2) it must be necessary to give business efficacy to the contract so that no term will be implied if the contract is effective without it;
(3) it must be so obvious that it goes without saying;
(4) it must be capable of clear expression; and
(5) it must not contradict any express term of the contract.[168]

252. The effect of Seepersad J.'s finding on this point, then, was that although there was a duty for the TTGF to be fair, there was no further duty owed by it to consult with Williams or her medical team prior to substituting her.

164. *Ibid.*, para. 17.
165. *Ibid.*, para. 15.
166. *Ibid.*, para. 108.
167. 1977 WL 165288.
168. *Thema Yakaena Williams v. Trinidad and Tobago Gymnastics Federation et al*-CV 2016-02608, para. 100.

253. Separate and apart from the question of implied contractual terms, though, the court still found that the TTGF breached its contract with Williams without justification.[169] The court's rationale was succinctly summarised at paragraphs 96 and 97 of the ruling:

> There existed a contractual relationship between the Claimant and the 1st Defendant, which gave rise to a duty to treat the Claimant fairly and/or reasonably and/or in good faith and/or to maintain impartiality and/or to avoid a partisan approach. This duty to act fairly had to be performed in circumstances in which the 1st Defendant had regulatory, disciplinary and coercive powers over gymnasts, including the Claimant. The TTGF also exercised exclusive and/or substantial control over the career and future of the Claimant as a participant in national and international events and in particular, her participation in the 2016 Olympics Test Event. The decision effected by and on behalf of the 1st Defendant on April 15, 2016 was characterized by a degree of Wednesbury unreasonableness and was a decision which should have never been taken.

254. The court, therefore, denounced the decision of the TTGF to replace her with Marisa Dick, when it considered the negative comments being made about Williams by the second to fifth Defendants as well as the alacrity with which the decision to substitute her was made. Seepersad J. stated that the Court 'formed the view that these Defendants allowed their entrenched biases to cloud their judgment and they acted with undue haste, deprived themselves of the benefit of relevant information and ultimately effected a flawed decision'.[170]

B. Breach of Fiduciary Duty

255. The disposition of this issue was fairly straightforward in view of the prevailing law that although fiduciary duties are owed by directors to a company, it is only where there is a special factual relationship would directors of a company owe a fiduciary duty to its members.[171] Seepersad J. observed that while the second to fifth defendants owed and breached their duty to the TTGF, there existed no individual or independent fiduciary duty by the Executive Committee members of the TTGF toward Williams.[172]

169. *Ibid.*, para. 98.
170. *Ibid.*, para. 94.
171. *Ibid.*, para. 117.
172. *Ibid.*, para. 125.

C. Procuring a Breach of Contract

256. As noted by the court in *Williams*,[173] the tort of procuring or inducing a breach of contract was established in *Lumley v. Gye.*[174] To establish the tort, there must be a direct inducement to breach the contract, while it must also be proven that: (i) the defendant knew of the existence of a contract, (ii) the defendant caused the breach of the contract and (iii) there was an intentional invasion of the rights of the claimant.[175]

257. On the facts of the current case, the onus lay on Williams to establish the above elements, in particular, the latter feature and she failed to do so. As a result, the court, somewhat easily, concluded that Williams' claim under this head lacked merit.[176]

D. Unlawful Means Conspiracy

258. The court in *Williams* cited the 2018 decision in *JSC BTA Bank v. Khrapunov*[177] in addressing the Claimant's plea that the second to fifth defendants conspired to use unlawful means to cause her injury. The court in *Khrapunov* tackled the question of unlawful means conspiracy in the following manner:

> The modern tort of conspiracy … is an anomalous tort because it may make actionable acts which would be lawful apart from the element of combination. The ostensible rationale, that acts done in combination are inherently more coercive than those done by a single actor, has not always been found persuasive, least of all when the single actor may be a powerful corporation … Nonetheless, the tort of conspiracy has an established place in the law of tort and its essential elements have been clarified by a series of modern decisions of high authority, most of them in contexts far removed from the modern tort's origin in the law relating to industrial disputes.
>
> It has been recognised since the decision of the House of Lords in *Quinn v Leathem [1901] AC 495* that the tort takes two forms: (i) conspiracy to injure, where the overt acts done pursuant to the conspiracy may be lawful but the predominant purpose is to injure the claimant; and (ii) conspiracy to do by unlawful means an act which may be lawful in itself, albeit that injury to the claimant is not the predominant purpose. In *Lonrho Plc v Fayed [1992] 1 AC 448*, Lord Bridge, with whom the rest of the Appellate Committee agreed, reviewed the earlier authorities and summarised the position as follows, at pp 465–466:

173. *Ibid.*, para. 129.
174. [1843-60] All ER Rep 208.
175. *Thema Yakaena Williams v. Trinidad and Tobago Gymnastics Federation et al*-CV 2016-02608, para. 130.
176. *Ibid.*, paras 135–136.
177. [2018] UKSC 19.

> Where conspirators act with the predominant purpose of injuring the plaintiff and in fact inflict damage on him, but do nothing which would have been actionable if done by an individual acting alone, it is in the fact of their concerted action for that illegitimate purpose that the law, however anomalous it may now seem, finds a sufficient ground to condemn their action as illegal and tortious. But when conspirators intentionally injure the plaintiff and use unlawful means to do so, it is no defence for them to show that their primary purpose was to further or protect their own interests; it is sufficient to make their action tortious that the means used were unlawful.[178]

259. This issue was not a complex one for the court in *Williams* to resolve. The court found that although the decision to replace Williams was unreasonable, premature, ill-advised and actuated by bias, it could not be said that the second to fifth defendants, as members of the TTGF's Executive Committee, had an intention to injure Williams. Further, the court concluded that, on the facts, it was difficult to find the existence of any conspiracy. As a result, this head of complaint was also found to be devoid of merit.[179]

260. In summary, therefore, liability was only found against the TTGF but not against the other four defendants. Williams was awarded approximately USD 30,000 in damages.

VI. The Failed FIFA Presidential Bid: David Nakhid

261. On 14 December 2015, the CAS rejected the candidacy of former Trinidad and Tobago standout David Nakhid, as he launched a bid to become the President of FIFA to replace Sepp Blatter in the elections scheduled for February 2016. In its media release, the CAS stated:

> In its decision of 28 October 2015, the FIFA AEC[180] found that Mr Nakhid had not presented declarations of support from at least five member associations, and for this reason, could not be admitted as a candidate for the election for the office of FIFA President on 26 February 2016 … In line with the FIFA AEC, the CAS Panel found that one member association had issued declarations of support to two candidates, including one for Mr Nakhid, in violation of the applicable FIFA rules. As a consequence, those letters of support were disregarded, meaning that David Nakhid had not met the qualifying criterion

178. *Ibid.*, at paras 7 and 8.
179. *Thema Yakaena Williams v. Trinidad and Tobago Gymnastics Federation et al*-CV 2016-02608, para. 147.
180. Ad hoc Electoral Committee.

of obtaining declarations of support from at least five member associations, and accordingly, his candidature could not be validated.[181]

262. No CAS award was published with regard to the *Nakhid* appeal so that the panel's reasons for its decision have not been made available to the public. One Trinidad-based media house, Wired868, nevertheless offered a useful summary of the proceedings:

> Nakhid's case essentially has two parts. First, the former Grasshoppers and New England Revolution midfielder and Caribbean Player of the Year argued that the Ad-hoc Electoral Committee violated the principle of transparency by inviting him to submit a letter of support from USVI, three days after it already received a letter from Champagne for the same member association.
>
> El Mir argued, on behalf of the Trinidadian, that: 'such (an) act is not only a violation of the integrity and transparency obligation of the Ad-hoc Committee, *but a clear manipulation of the election process*, by intriguing Mr. Nakhid into a disqualification situation, for an act that he is absolutely not personally responsible of (sic).' ... In its written response to CAS, FIFA sought to dismiss the suggestion that it had entrapped Nakhid and played an active role in his subsequent disqualification ... The governing body further insisted that it had no obligation to warn Nakhid of a potential invalidation under its electoral regulations and pointed to the final sentence of Article 13.1 (c), which states: 'If a member association presents declarations of support for more than one person, all its declarations shall become invalid.'
>
> 'Through this clear provision, legal certainty, predictability of decisions as well as equal treatment of all candidates is ensured,' stated FIFA. 'A duty of the FIFA Ad-hoc Electoral Committee to advise any of the two candidates in context with letters of support (...) is not contained [in] the FIFA Statutes and/or any FIFA regulations.'[182] [Emphasis original]

263. This case appears to have had the potential to impact significantly on football governance both locally and internationally, with the interpretation of the FIFA Statutes and electoral regulations in view. It is also well known that the inherent confidentiality of arbitration proceedings can only be waived with the parties' consent so that it was not mandatory for the CAS to make this award available to the public. Yet, notwithstanding the dismissal of Nakhid's appeal, the case was a reminder of the central role played by arbitration in the resolution of sporting disputes, including high-profile conflicts.

---

181. Media Release FIFA Presidential Election, The CAS dismisses the Appeal of David Nakhid, 14 Dec. 2015.

182. Lasana Liburd, *FIFA v. Nakhid: The Shocking Truth of their CAS battle and why it matters*, 28 Dec. 2015, https://wired868.com/2015/12/28/fifa-versus-nakhid-the-shocking-truth-of-their-cas-battle-and-why-it-matters/.

VII. Sports Arbitration in Trinidad and Tobago: General Comments

264. Over five years ago it was noted that Qatar was 'in the process of modernising its law on arbitration. It is expected the new rules, again based on the UNCITRAL Model Law, will be passed shortly … Aside from the World Cup … there has been a clear shift in favour of arbitration in domestic disputes because it is recognised as a more expedient process'.[183]

265. It is indisputable that arbitration has evolved into a favoured mechanism for the extra-judicial settlement of disputes. Just a few years before the 2022 World Cup, Qatar, as host nation, is refining its ADR framework as are many of its Middle Eastern neighbours, whose increasing prowess in trade and economy has necessitated such initiatives.

266. In the Caribbean, the journey is still very much at the early stages given the ad hoc nature of sports dispute resolution processes. At present, arbitration has been centred primarily on conflicts in cricket, with no new or established ADR entity having developed a lucid, well-structured framework for managing sports-related disputes, as the CAS and others like Just Sport Ireland, Sport Resolutions UK or the Sports Tribunal of New Zealand have so successfully done.

267. In Trinidad and Tobago, sporadic sports-based arbitrations have been the norm and while the above-mentioned High Court decisions have offered a useful starting point in discerning how arbitration law and principles can be applied to the sports sector, this country still awaits a coherent legal, academic and practical foundation that would give sports arbitration, the credibility and sustainability that the industry really needs.

---

183. *The Resolver*, August 2013, p. 7.

Part II. Sport and Employment

Chapter 1. General Issues

268. One of the clear effects of the commercialisation of the global sports industry has been the steady increase in employment opportunities in the sector, whether as professional athletes, managers, agents or educators. A direct consequence of this ever-growing commercialisation is that there is a greater awareness of legal rights and responsibilities on the part of employers and employees alike.

269. In Trinidad and Tobago, the vast majority of NGBs are serviced by volunteers with very few remunerated full-time staff. Notably, all three sports of focus in this monograph have paid staff as part of their employment structure. These are:

(1) the office of the Secretary of the NAAATT;
(2) the office of the Secretary General of the TTFA; and
(3) the office of the Chief Executive Officer of the TTCB.

270. The largest number of employees within the sports industry in Trinidad and Tobago is found within the public sector, with an approximate combined staff of about 350 persons at the MSYA and the SPORTT. Beyond the public sector, one can find a sustainable employment structure in the field of sports education.

271. As mentioned in Part I of this monograph, the St. Augustine Campus of the UWI in Trinidad and Tobago offers a number of sports-based undergraduate and post-graduate degrees from the Faculty of Social Sciences[184] with these programmes employing full-time and adjunct lecturers. For example, in January 2018 the Faculty of Law introduced Commonwealth Caribbean Sports Law as a third year elective module for law students. While these educational programmes seem to lay the foundation for future careers in sport, even qualified students in Trinidad and Tobago struggle to find employment in the sports sector after completing their academic pursuits.

272. On the field of play, there has been a slow but steady increase in sports participants plying their trade like professionals. This has happened in football, through

184. These are primarily Sports Management degrees, while there is also a FIFA/UWI/CIES post-graduate diploma in Sports Management.

the Trinidad and Tobago Professional Football League as well as in regional cricket under the auspices of CWI and to a lesser extent domestically under the TTCB.

273. However, there seems to be a greater incidence of professional sportspersons in individual sports such as swimming, golf, non-team events in track and field, boxing, table-tennis, tennis, rifle shooting, body-building, weightlifting, taekwondo, judo, gymnastics and archery.

274. Very few cases have emanated from Trinidad and Tobago involving industrial or labour relations, although, at the regional level there have been a number of cricket-based cases that have gone to arbitration and the Supreme Court.

275. In the next chapter, we will examine more closely the broader context of sports-related employment including some cases that have been ventilated in the courts of Trinidad and Tobago.

Chapter 2. Sources of Employment Law

§1. Introduction

276. Except for Guyana and St. Lucia, most Caribbean countries, including Trinidad and Tobago, have been strongly influenced by English common law.[185] In fact, the common law combined with legislation represents a primary source of law in Trinidad and Tobago, including employment law.

277. Sources of law in the Caribbean can be divided into two broad categories: (i) formal sources and (ii) informal sources.[186] The formal sources are:

- the Common Law;
- legislation;
- codes of Practice;
- CARICOM instruments;
- international law; and
- the International Labour Organization, its Conventions, Recommendations and Codes of Practice.

278. The informal sources are:

- custom and practice;
- collective Labour Agreements; and
- work Rules.[187]

279. In the context of sport in Trinidad and Tobago, the influence of the common law, legislation, CARICOM instruments, international law and Collective Labour Agreements as sources of law, has been more pronounced.

§2. The Legal Basis of the Employment Relationship

280. O' Leary's[188] synopsis of the employment relationship provides a sound building block for assessing employment contracts in the sports industry. From a British perspective she noted that the 'basis for an employment relationship in the United Kingdom is an employment contract. The tests for establishing whether an employment contract (or a contract of service as it is frequently termed) exists are prescribed in common law'. She added that if 'an employment contract does not

---

185. This chapter includes an amended and updated version of an article entitled 'Law, Labour and the West Indies Player: A recent history of contractual and governance disputes' which was first published in the June 2016 edition of the *Global Sports Law and Taxation Reports*.
186. Natalie Corthésy and Carla-Anne Harris-Roper, *Commonwealth Caribbean Employment and Labour Law* 17 (Routledge 2014).
187. *Ibid.*, Ch. 2.
188. Leanne O'Leary, *Employment and Labour Relations in the Premier League, NBA and the International Rugby Union* (2017, Springer).

exist, a party may be considered in law as a worker or self-employed. The advantage of employee status is that it entitles a person to minimum statutory employment rights for which an independent contractor or worker may not be eligible. Employee status is also relevant for issues of vicarious liability under tort law, the application of trade union law, health and safety legislation and tax law'.[189]

281. In other words, the definition of who is an employee has legal and practical consequences, with predictable variations depending on the governing law that forms the backdrop for the interpretation of the diverse contractual terms and provisions.

§3. The Legal Status of Players

282. Commensurate with O'Leary's analysis, the situation in Trinidad and Tobago is that the legal relationship between professional athletes and their employers is based on the law of contract. Of the three main sports under closer scrutiny in this monograph, football has made the greatest strides in formalising a detailed contractual framework for professional footballers as seen in the contents of the Players' Agreement that is embedded in the Handbook of the Trinidad and Tobago Professional Football League (also known as the TT Pro League Handbook).[190]

283. As far as cricket is concerned, the functions of the CBA and Memorandum of Understanding (MOU) are fundamental in determining the status of Trinidad and Tobago cricketers that have played for the West Indies (now known as the 'Windies') cricket team. Athletics, however, is understandably different given the individual nature of this sport. The following sections of this chapter focus exclusively on employment law in the context of football.

§4. The Footballer in Trinidad and Tobago

284. The TT Pro League Handbook defines 'Player' as 'any Contract Player, Out of Contract Player, Non-Contract Player, Trainee or Student who plays or is eligible to play for a Club'.[191] Each of these terms has been specifically defined:

(1) 'Contract Player' means 'any player (other than a Trainee or Apprentice) who is eligible to play under a written contract of employment with a Club'.
(2) 'Out of Contract Player' means 'a Contract Player whose contract has expired'.

---

189. *Ibid.*, p. 89.
190. The handbook consists of the Rules of the TT Pro League, together with three appendices and various supplementary documents like players' contracts and Codes of Conduct for Managers and Clubs.
191. Section A (Introduction), p. 3.

(3) 'Non-Contract Player' means 'any Player (other than a Trainee or an Apprentice) who is eligible to play for a Club with which he has not entered into a written contract of employment'.
(4) 'Trainee' means 'a Player of the age of 16, 17 or 18 years registered by a Club'.
(5) 'Student' means 'a player playing in age groups Under 9–18 who is coached by or at or playing football for or at a Football Academy or a Centre of Excellence'.
(6) 'Club' means 'an association football club in membership of the League'.

285. The above definitions reflect an attempt by the TT Pro League to capture all levels of footballers in the country, therefore encompassing amateur and professional players. It is instructive to note that these Rules and Regulations recognised the centrality of the contract of employment in determining the status of the footballer. The absence of an employment contract causes the player to fall into the category of either 'Out-of-Contract' or 'Non-Contract'.

286. One question that arises, then, is if similar criteria were to be used in other sports what classification would be afforded to self-employed athletes like tennis players, boxers, golfers or rifle shooters. Herein lies the difference between individual sports and team sports, a feature that is germane to global sport.

I. The Employment Relationship

287. As seen above, the definition of a 'Contract Player' in the TT Pro League Handbook is predicated upon the existence of a contract of employment. The Handbook[192] proceeds to provide a contractual template entitled the Trinidad & Tobago Pro League Contract, which contains twenty-seven clauses. It is noteworthy that the contract contains no sub-headings before the Schedule but instead is drafted as one full document. Some of the key clauses will be examined below.

II. Fundamental Rights and Obligations for Clubs and Players

288. The footballer's obligations dominate the first half of the contract and include the following commitments and undertakings:

- To play to the best of his ability in all football matches in which he is selected to play for the Club.
- To attend at any reasonable place for the purpose of training.
- To attend all matches in which the Club is engaged.

---

192. Form 11 of the TT Pro League Handbook.

- To play football solely and exclusively for his employing Club as authorised by the Club or as required under the Rules of the TTFF[193] and the Rules of the Trinidad and Tobago Pro League.
- To adhere to the Laws of the Game of Association Football in all matches in which he participates.
- To observe the rules of his employing Club at all times.
- To refrain from participating professionally in any other sporting or athletic activity without the written consent of his employing Club.
- To have due regard for the necessity of maintaining a high standard of physical fitness.
- To avoid indulging in any sport, activity or practice that might endanger such fitness.
- To be available for community and public relations involvement at reasonable times during the period of the contract.
- To report to his employing club any incapacity or sickness.
- To allow himself to be photographed by his employing club as a member of the squad of players.
- To make media contributions in a responsible manner generally, and specifically in a way that does not bring the game of association football into disrepute.
- To refrain from inducing or attempting to induce any other footballer from his own club or from another Club to terminate that player's contract of employment.[194]
- To avoid residing in a location which his employing club deems unsuitable for the performance of his duties under his employment contract.

289. As far as the employing club's obligations are concerned, the TT Pro League contract lists only a few undertakings:

(1) To provide players, at the earliest opportunity, with copies of all relevant *Trinidad and Tobago Football Federation Rules, Trinidad and Tobago Pro League Rules* or Club Rules together with any relevant insurance policy.
(2) To promptly arrange medical treatment, including dental treatment, in the case of a player's incapacity or illness, without attaching expense for same to the respective player.
(3) To afford players every opportunity compatible with their obligations under their contract of employment to pursue courses of further education or vocational training.

290. It is not a unique feature of the TT Pro League contract that the obligations of the player are more rigorous than those of the Club. A quick overview of the foregoing obligations highlights a clear disparity in the legal obligations of employer and employee. The termination clauses appear to be an attempt to level the playing field somewhat.

193. Now known as the TTFA.
194. These 14 obligations are found in Clauses 1–14 of the TT Pro League Contract.

III. The Termination Clauses in the TT Pro League Contract

291. A footballer's contract may be terminated in accordance with Clause 16 of the TT Pro League Contract, which states, in part, as follows:

> If the Player shall be guilty of serious or persistent misconduct or serious or persistent breach of the Rules of the Club or the terms and conditions of this Agreement the Club may on giving fourteen days' written notice to the Player terminate this Agreement in accordance with the Rules of the Trinidad & Tobago Football Federation and the Rules of the Trinidad and Tobago Pro League and the Club shall notify the Player in writing of the full reasons for the action taken. Such action shall be subject to the player's right of appeal …

292. No explanation is offered as to what exactly constitutes 'serious or persistent misconduct' or 'serious or persistent breach'. It can only be assumed that any adjudicatory panel sitting to determine whether a termination has been lawful or not will be guided by some standard or threshold upon which to measure the propriety of the footballer's behaviour.

293. On the other hand, a footballer can trigger termination of his employment with his Club in accordance with Clause 17 of the TT Pro League Contract, which states, in part, as follows: 'If the Club is guilty of serious or persistent breach of the terms and conditions of this agreement the Player may on giving fourteen days written notice to the Club terminate this agreement.' Clause 17 goes on further to establish that the Club has a right of appeal, with both Club and player having a further right of appeal. The first level of appeal for either party is to the Board of the Trinidad and Tobago Pro League, while the second level of appeal is to the Appeals Committee of the TTFF.

294. Again, no explanation has been given as to what constitutes a 'serious or persistent breach' of the employment contract by the Club. This scenario of a player initiating termination due to the Club's breach has been virtually absent in Trinidad and Tobago's football history and is, perhaps, not surprising given the unequal bargaining power between player and Club generally.

IV. The Disciplinary Clauses

295. The TT Pro League Handbook contemplates situations where a player's conduct falls short of that which warrants termination but, at least, deserves some form of punitive measures being imposed. Clause 18 captures this in the following words: 'If the Player is guilty of misconduct or a breach of any of the training or disciplinary rules or lawful instructions of the Club or any of the provisions of this Agreement the Club may either impose a fine not exceeding two weeks' basic wages or order the Player not to attend at the Club for a period not exceeding fourteen days. The Club shall inform the Player in writing of the action taken and the full reasons for it …'

296. Clause 18 appears to have as its objective, punishing lesser offences, that is to say, conduct that is not as severe as to justify termination of the employment contract. In this regard, it speaks to a breach of training rules, disciplinary rules, lawful Club instructions or any provisions of the contract. The main distinction between Clause 18 and Clause 16 (The Termination Clause) is the removal of the words 'serious or persistent' in Clause 18. Both clauses punish a breach of the contractual terms and conditions, but only a serious or persistent breach will result in termination.

297. The termination of the contract of former national goalkeeper, Jan-Michael Williams from W Connection Football Club in 2013 did not result in litigation. Media reports only spoke about an amicable split between the parties. An excerpt from an online article from one media entity put it this way: 'There will be no reconciliation for defending Pro League champion football club DIRECTV W Connection and its former team captain and custodian Jan-Michael Williams. But there will be no more accusations from the two parties either. W Connection chairman David John Williams and his namesake and former employee, Williams-the two are not related-told *Wired868* last night that they would essentially agree to disagree and part amicably. W Connection will continue to pay Williams, who is also the Trinidad and Tobago national football team captain, until his contract expires in March.'[195]

298. It appears that the trigger for the disagreement that eventually ended Williams' employment relationship with W Connection was a falling out during a team video session in which the goalkeeper took offence to what the media described as 'colourful language' used by the team's coach during the session. Williams walked out of the team meeting which the coach interpreted as an undermining of his authority.[196]

299. W Connection is a Club participating in the TT Pro League and its players would, like those of the other Clubs, have signed the above-mentioned TT Pro League contract, mutatis mutandis. The question then begs whether Williams' conduct constituted 'serious or persistent misconduct' or 'serious or persistent breach' deserving of termination. The factual context, though, suggests that even before the termination clause could be triggered, some sort of settlement agreement was reached.

195. Lasana Liburd, *Connection and Jan-Michael agree amicable split*, https://wired868.com/2013/01/18/connection-and-jan-michael-agree-amicable-split/, 18 Jan. 2013.
196. *Ibid.*

300. On the issue of conduct that falls short of deserving termination, the provisions of the TT Pro League contract must be read in tandem with the relevant sections of the TT Pro League Handbook. Section P of the latter deals with inquiries, commissions and appeals with section P.4, in particular, stating that '[e]xcept in the case of those Rules in respect of which a fixed penalty for breach is prescribed, any suspected or alleged breach of these Rules may be dealt with by a commission established by the Board'.

301. One of the commissions established by the TT Pro League is its Disciplinary Committee. This commission, like others, must be chaired by legally qualified persons.[197] A range of potential sanctions has also been made available to the commissions such as a reprimand, fine, suspension, deduction of points, expulsion or other penalty or any combination of the foregoing.[198] In the case of expulsion of a club from the league, a special resolution must be passed at a general meeting of the league authorising same. It is axiomatic that any disciplinary measure applied must pass the test of proportionality.

302. Recently, in *CAS 2017/A/5003 Jérôme Valcke v. FIFA*, the CAS offered the following useful guidance:

> There is well-recognized CAS jurisprudence to the effect that whenever an association uses its discretion to impose a sanction, CAS will have regard to that association's expertise but, if having done so, the CAS panel considers nonetheless that the sanction is disproportionate, it must, given its *de novo* powers of review, be free to say so and apply the appropriate sanction.

303. The above represents a re-statement of the well-established proportionality principle that is recognised in national law, both criminal and civil, and in sports law jurisprudence.

304. Disputes involving Clubs, Officials and Players must be referred to the TTFF for resolution, unless the Pro League Rules say otherwise.[199] In this capacity it appears that the TTFF acts as a dispute resolution tribunal. However, there is a separate Football Federation Appeals Committee which sits as an appellate body to hear appeals from decisions made or penalties imposed by the Board of a Commission established under section P.4.

305. It may very well be prudent for the current football administrators in Trinidad and Tobago to consider the establishment of a body similar to the FIFA Dispute Resolution Chamber (DRC) to hear and determine football-related disputes.

197. TT Pro League Handbook, s. p. 3.3.
198. *Ibid.*, s. P.7.1.
199. *Ibid.*, s. P.8.

Such an entity may be able to serve the Pro League, the Trinidad and Tobago Super League, the Secondary Schools Football League (SSFL) and the various other zonal associations affiliated with the TTFA.

306. A good example of the usefulness of the FIFA DRC was the CAS ruling in *Kedah Football Association v. Adriano Pelligrino.*[200] One of the issues arising in this case was whether the FIFA DRC had jurisdiction to hear the matter. The CAS Panel referred to one of the employment contracts entered into by the footballer Pelligrino under which the parties 'had agreed to resort to internal dispute resolution mechanisms before filing the case at FIFA'.[201]

307. The salient clause was Clause 8 of the Mutual Termination Agreement which stated that '[i]f there is any dispute or if the Club or the Player fails to comply with the Agreement, the matter shall be referred to the FIFA Dispute Resolution Chamber'.[202] The CAS Panel found that the FIFA DRC had correctly asserted its jurisdiction,[203] at the same time, reinforcing the status of the DRC as a credible ADR mechanism for the resolution of football-related disputes.

V. Player Transfers

308. Commendably, the TT Pro League Handbook dedicates an entire section[204] to address player transfers. Undoubtedly, the Bosman[205] decision had an effect that surpassed European borders with Trinidad and Tobago players, such as goalkeeping standout and ESPN football analyst Shaka Hislop, benefitting from that seminal 1995 ruling from the European Court of Justice.

309. It is a well-recorded fact that the *Bosman* decision radically transformed the transfer system not only in European football but also in global football as a whole. Jean-Marc Bosman, a Belgian footballer sought a transfer to French club US Dunkerque at the end of his contract with RC Liège. The transfer never materialised after Liège failed to request an International Transfer Certificate from the Belgian Football Federation, a pre-condition for a lawful transfer. Liège's reticence to facilitate the transfer was based on its doubts as to Dunkerque's solvency when the transfer fee was agreed.

310. Bosman's subsequent suspension by Liège left him without employment, a fact which his legal representative was able to highlight as contrary to EU law.

---

200. CAS 2015/A/4358, award of 13 May 2016.
201. *Ibid.*, para. 62.
202. *Ibid.*, para. 65.
203. *Ibid.*, para. 66.
204. Section L.
205. *Union Royale Belge des Sociétés de Football Association ASBL v. Jean-Marc Bosman*, Case C-415/93, [1995] ECR I-4921.

Advocate General Lenz agreed and, ultimately, the then European Court of Justice[206] concluded that it was unlawful for an employee who was an EU national to be hindered from plying his trade, due to a restriction which was not objectively justifiable. Thus, the end-of-contract transfer fee was abolished.

311. The applicable transfer rules in the TT Pro League Handbook are fairly comprehensive. Section L.12 is worded in a manner that suggests that *Bosman* lessons have been learned in Trinidad and Tobago. That portion of section L.12 addresses Out-of-Contract players. It says, in part, as follows:

> Provided that the following conditions are satisfied, a Compensation Fee shall be paid to a Transferor Club by a Transferee Club on the transfer of the registration of an Out of Contract Player:
> the Out of Contract Player in question must be under the age of 23 years[207];
>> on or after the date of the Transfer Deadline and on or before the third Saturday in November in the year in which the player's contract is to expire or, in the circumstances mentioned in Rule K.25, within 4 days of the last relevant Football Federation Cup match or League Match in that year having been played, the Transferor Club must send to the Player Form 22 offering a new contract on the terms therein set out, which must be *no less favourable than those in his current contract*[208] [Emphasis added]

312. Section L.13 adds further clarity in stating that contract terms 'shall be deemed to be no less favourable if, disregarding any provision for a Signing-on-Fee[209] in the player's current contract which is stated to be a once only payment, they are at least equal in value to the most favourable terms to which the Player was or is entitled in any year of his current contract'.

313. A number of features of this Rule stand out. First, as mentioned above, an 'Out of Contract Player' is defined in section A of the TT Pro League Handbook as 'a Contract Player whose contract has expired', while a 'Contract Player' is 'any player (other than a Trainee or Apprentice) who is eligible to play under a written contract of employment with a Club'. Section L.12, then, seeks to protect future 'Bosmans' who have come to the end of their playing contract.

206. Now the Court of Justice of the European Union (CJEU).
207. Section L 12.1.
208. Section L 12.2.
209. 'Signing-on Fee' is defined in Section A of the TT Pro League Handbook as 'a lump sum payment payable under the terms of a contract between a Club and a Contract Player.'

314. Second, the reference to the new contract of an Out of Contract player not being on less favourable terms appears to be a direct allusion to the factual background in the *Bosman* decision where Bosman was being offered a monthly salary of BFR 30,000 for a one-year renewal by Liège, when his previous salary was BFR 120,000 including bonuses.[210]

315. The reference to Form 22 in section L.12.2 is a reference to a template document called the Trinidad and Tobago Pro League Offer of a New Contract. Notably, the template closes using the following clause:

> This offer remains open and capable of acceptance for a period of one month within which time you may either accept it and enter into a new contract in the terms offered or decline it in writing. If you consider that the terms offered are less favourable than those in your current contract you may give notice to that effect in the Application for Free Transfer (Form 23).

316. Form 22, therefore, which gives practical effect to section L.14, seems to be an attempt to maintain some level of contractual balance in circumstances where bargaining power typically tends to favour the employing Club. Form 23 is another template document which reflects the provisions of section L.15 which states that: 'If the Player considers that the terms offered by his Club and set out in Form 22 are less favourable than those in his current contract, he may give notice to that effect to his Club and the Secretary in Form 23 and apply for a free transfer.'

317. In other words, an Out of Contract Player at the end of his existing contract with a football club in the TT Pro League has, at least, three options:

> Option 1: to accept, within one month, the offer of a new contract from his current Club as long as the terms of the new contract are no less favourable than those in the current contract.
> Option 2: to decline the offer of the new contract from his current club.
> Option 3: to apply for a free transfer, if he holds the view that the contractual terms in the new contract are less favourable than those in his current contract.[211] Any such application for a free transfer must be approved by the Pro League Board.[212]

318. Notably, if the application for a free transfer is indeed successful, two consequences ensue. First, the player's current club (the Transferor Club) will not be

210. *Union Royale Belge des Sociétés de Football Association ASBL v. Jean-Marc Bosman*, Case C-415/93, [1995] ECR I-4921 at paras 28–29.
211. Section L.15, TT Pro League Handbook/Rules.
212. *Ibid.*, s. L.16.

entitled to a compensation fee[213] when the player's registration is transferred.[214] Second, the footballer will receive severance pay in accordance with Rule L.21.[215]

319. From an employment law perspective, Rule L.21 is significant. It states:

> For a period of one month after the expiry of his contract, or (if earlier) until his registration is transferred to a Transferee Club,[216] an Out of Contract Player who has received no offer under Rule L.12.2 or who has succeeded in an application under Rule L.15 shall be entitled to receive from his Club by way of severance payment the weekly basic wage under his expired contract or, if his registration is transferred within the one month period, any amount by which the weekly basic wage payable to him by the Transferee Club in the remainder of that period falls short of the weekly basic wage payable under the expired contract.

320. In Trinidad and Tobago, the Retrenchment and Severance Benefits Act Chapter 88.13[217] is one in an inventory of statutes that affects the livelihood of employed persons. This statute is of particular interest from a sporting perspective in view of the various related definitions around who is an employee or worker.

321. These are a few of the relevant definitions:

(1) 'casual worker' means a person who is employed on a temporary or on an irregular or intermittent basis;
(2) 'independent contractor' means a person who is engaged on the basis of a contractual arrangement to do work over an estimated period of time and whose hours of work are not regulated by contract;
(3) 'seasonal worker' means a person who is regularly employed each year, but not throughout the year, to perform work which is limited to a certain time or certain times of the year because of the seasonal nature of the work involved;
(4) 'worker' means a worker within the meaning of the Industrial Relations Act.

322. The definition of worker' in the Industrial Relations Act Chapter 88:01[218] is a detailed one. Subsection (a) suffices, however, when considering the status of professional footballers in Trinidad and Tobago. A 'worker' subject to subsection (3)

213. The 'Compensation Fee' is defined in s. A of the TT Pro League Rules as 'any sum of money (exclusive of Value Added Tax) payable by a Transferee Club to a Transferor Club upon the transfer of the registration of a player'.
214. Rule L.16.1, TT Pro League Rules.
215. Rule L.16.2, TT Pro League Rules.
216. 'Transferee Club' is defined in Section A of the TT Pro League Rules as 'a Club (or a club) to which the registration of a Player is, or is to be or has been transferred.' In other words, this is the receiving club. 'Transferor Club' or the sending club, is defined as 'a Club (or a club) from which the registration of a Player is, or is to be or has been transferred.'
217. Act No. 32 of 1985.
218. Act No. 23 of 1972.

of the Industrial Relations Act means 'any person who has entered into or works under a contract with an employer to do any skilled, unskilled, manual, technical, clerical or other work for hire or reward, whether the contract is expressed or implied, oral or in writing, or partly oral and partly in writing, and whether it is a contract of service or apprenticeship or a contract personally to execute any work or labour'. A Contract Player in the TT Pro League, then, is a 'worker' for the purposes of the Industrial Relations Act.

323. This array of definitions from the foregoing statutes has not been judicially tested in a sporting context in Trinidad and Tobago, although the various terms have been considered in a series of trade disputes over many years.

324. The definition of 'casual worker' in the Retrenchment and Severance Benefits Act appears to capture at least one category of footballer in the TT Pro League. The Pro League Rules mention the 'Week by Week Contract' which refers to a playing contract between a Club and a Player which is terminated by either party on seven days' written notice.[219] The name of the contract may be somewhat misleading as it suggests that the duration of the playing contract is only for one week. What seems more plausible, though, is for the contract to be of longer duration but it can be brought to an end by one week's notice.

325. The question begs, then, whether a footballer who is hired, perhaps, for the last three months of the season, will be a 'casual worker' for the purposes of the Retrenchment and Severance Benefits Act. Such a player may even be classed as a 'seasonal worker' given the fact that his employment is not throughout the year, but it is unlikely that Parliament intended to include that type of worker.

326. No footballer appearing before the Industrial Court of Trinidad and Tobago is likely to successfully claim that he or she is an independent contractor since that player's hours of work are regulated. A boxer, golfer, tennis player, table-tennis player or rifle shooter may have greater interpretive success in that regard, especially if the contract being construed is one with an agent or manager. Yet, legally speaking, a more accurate description of the status of those persons plying their trade in individual sports is that of a self-employed worker, as compared to an independent contractor.

327. Lewis and Taylor have noted the dilemma that an individual sport like boxing poses:

> A boxer is also, in strict legal terms, the principal in his relationship with his manager, but this relationship is of a different order: the boxer is often the subordinate party. In reality a manager will control the boxers who 'employ' him and they will depend on him for work (ie by arranging fights via contracts with others) and hence remuneration. The relationship is more akin to the manager as employer and the boxer as employee … As such, a boxer is more reliant on

219. Section A.

his agent than, for example, professional golfers, snooker players and tennis players (who may also employ agents). The latter generally have more economic independence and are more obviously self-employed professional sportsmen.[220]

328. The question of self-employed professional does not arise, generally speaking, in team sports like cricket and football so that, as noted above, for the purposes of both the Retrenchment and Severance Benefits Act and The Industrial Relations Act in Trinidad and Tobago, the Pro League footballer is a 'worker'. Although no definition of 'severance payment' is found in the former Act, section L.15 of the Pro League Rules attempts to compensate the Out of Contract Player who is applying for a free transfer with some form of remuneration. Prima facie, this appears to be a post-Bosman benefit being applied in a Trinidad and Tobago context. A brief word on the main Bosman transfers for Trinidad and Tobago's footballers is opportune.

VI. Bosman Transfers

329. Former national goalkeeper and captain Shaka Hislop remains one of the highest profile footballers to ever play for Trinidad and Tobago. Perhaps Dwight Yorke, Russell Latapy, David Nakhid and Kenwyne Jones are his only compatriots to have played professional football at the same levels as Hislop. Hislop's transfers between August 1998 and July 2006 were all post-Bosman free transfers. The foregoing transfers, save one, were all in the English Premier League first from Newcastle to West Ham in 1998, West Ham to Portsmouth in 2002, Portsmouth back to West Ham in 2005, and finally in 2006 from West Ham to Major League Soccer's (MLS) Dallas FC[221] in the United States (US).[222]

330. Former Aston Villa and Manchester United standout Dwight Yorke's only free transfer occurred in 2005 when he moved from his then employers Birmingham to Sydney FC in Australia.[223] Russell Latapy, like Hislop, also benefitted from four free transfers while he played in Europe. Between 1998 and 2004 he moved from Boavista in Portugal to Hibernian FC in Scotland in 1998, within Scotland from Hibernian to Rangers in 2001, with a further two internal Scottish transfers from Rangers to Dundee United in 2003 and finally from Dundee United to Falkirk FC in 2004.[224]

331. Unlike the other three footballers, Kenwyne Jones' free transfers were not consecutive. Three such transfers occurred, the first one taking place notably when

220. Adam Lewis QC and Jonathan Taylor (now Jonathan Taylor QC), *Sport: Law and Practice* 1330 (Bloomsbury 3d ed., 2014), at para. H 1.4.
221. https://www.transfermarkt.com/shaka-hislop/transfers/spieler/4175.
222. Hislop retired from professional football in August 2007 while at Dallas FC.
223. https://www.transfermarkt.co.uk/dwight-yorke/transfers/spieler/3223.
224. Latapy retired from professional football in 2009 while at Falkirk FC.

he left Trinidad and Tobago's W Connection Football Club to move to Southampton in the English Premier League in 2004. His next free transfer did not occur until ten years later when in 2014 he moved from Stoke City to Cardiff. After a few loans, which took him to Bournemouth and Al-Jazira[225] and then back to Cardiff, Jones' final free transfer was from Cardiff to Atlanta United in the MLS.

332. Another footballer who played within European circles was goalkeeper Kelvin Jack. Interestingly, both Jack and Hislop represented Trinidad and Tobago at their historic debut appearance at the 2006 FIFA World Cup in Germany. Jack, however, became known not only for his exploits on the field of play but perhaps even more for his successful legal challenge to the conduct of his agent, Imageview Management Ltd, when he was transferring from Reading FC in England to Dundee United in Scotland.

VII. *Imageview Management Ltd v. Kelvin Jack*: Regulating Agents

333. The regulation of football agents has had a colourful global history, especially given their sometimes controversial reputation. Nevertheless, there is little disagreement that their role is a significant one in the life of a professional athlete.

334. Lewis and Taylor have offered a succinct synopsis of the agent's duties:

> Players' agents perform a variety of services for sportsmen and women (and clubs). Their principal role is in brokering, advising on and negotiating player transfers and contracts of employment … But players' agents also perform many tasks around the periphery of this activity, including the sourcing of endorsement deals and the provision of legal advice, as well as advice on financial planning, image rights exploitation and tax.[226]

335. In the cut and thrust of the modern sports industry with complex commercial contracts and lucrative sponsorship, endorsement and image rights agreements, it is hard to envision a professional sportsman or sportswomen operating without an agent, especially if that agent has legal qualifications.

336. The TTFA has been forward thinking enough to write regulations addressing agents. Section P 1.1 of the Pro League Rules defines an 'agent' in the following way:

> 'Agent' means a person who for reward represents, negotiates on behalf of, [or] otherwise acts for a Principal in the context of either:
>
> 1.1.1 the transfer of a Player's registration; or

225. A football club from Abu Dhabi in the United Arab Emirates.
226. Lewis and Taylor, *supra*, n. 220, at 1419, para. H 3.2.

1.1.2 the terms of a contract between a Player and a Club; or
1.1.3 the terms of a contract between a Manager and a Club;

337. Further, the 'Licensed Agent' means 'an agent to whom a licence has been granted under the provisions of this Section of these Rules or a corporation managed or controlled by such Agent'. The Rules continue by defining a 'FIFA Licensed Agent' as one 'to whom a licence has been granted under the provisions of the FIFA Regulations Governing Players' Agents'. Notably, 'Principal' means a Club, a Manager, an Official or a Player employing an Agent in any of the contexts referred to above.

338. Bowstead & Reynolds on Agency[227] defines agency at common law as follows:

> Agency is the fiduciary relationship which exists between two persons, one of whom expressly or impliedly consents that the other should act on his behalf so as to affect his relations with third parties, and the other of whom similarly consents so to act or so acts. The one on whose behalf the act or acts are to be done is called the principal. The one who is to act is called the agent. Any person other than the principal and the agent may be referred to as a third party.[228]

339. In short, the agent acts on behalf of the principal in a fiduciary relationship. The common law imposes the following key duties on agents:

(1) to act in accordance with the terms of appointment and not to exceed authority;
(2) to obey instructions given by the principal;
(3) to use due skill and care;
(4) to avoid and to make full disclosure as to potential conflicts of interest;
(5) not to make a secret profit;
(6) to keep the principal's property separate and to preserve correct accounts;
(7) to carry out instructions with reasonable dispatch.[229]

340. The Pro League Rules have, therefore, adopted a narrower function of agents based on its definitions, but still capture the central functions on representation and negotiation. There is comfort, therefore, for principals in Trinidad and Tobago given the broader common law duties.

---

227. 17th ed. (Sweet and Maxwell 2001).
228. *Ibid.*, at p. 1. This definition is based partly on what is known as the American *Restatement*.
229. Lewis and Taylor, *supra*, n. 220, at 1422–1424, paras H 3.10–H 3.18.

341. Such comfort was needed when former 2006 World Cup goalkeeper, Trinidad and Tobago's Kelvin Jack sought a transfer from Reading FC to Dundee United. In *Imageview Management Ltd. v. Jack,*[230] the duty of football agents was brought under close judicial scrutiny.

342. At the material time, Jack was employed with Reading Football Club in England and was interested in moving to Scotland to continue plying his trade. Through his agent, Mike Berry, who himself provided his agency services through Imageview Management Ltd, Jack successfully transferred to the Scottish team, Dundee United Football Club.

343. As a non-EU national, Jack needed to secure a work permit which Berry accomplished on his behalf. Yet, unknown to Jack, Berry also concluded a secret agreement with Dundee, in which he was paid GBP 3,000. Jack eventually found out about the side deal and when he confronted Berry, was told quite brashly that it was none of his business.

344. After this fallout, Jack stopped paying the commission due to Berry under the agency agreement, which non-payment became the subject matter of the litigation commenced by Imageview. In finding for Jack in this regard, the court expounded on the core role and function of an agent in unforgettable language:

> The law imposes on agents high standards. Footballers' agents are not exempt from these. An agent's own personal interests come entirely second to the interest of his client. If you undertake to act for a man, you must act 100%, body and soul, for him. You must act as if you were him. You must not allow your own interest to get in the way without telling him. An undisclosed but realistic possibility of a conflict of interest is a breach of your duty of good faith to your client.[231]

345. The court, then, did not necessarily frown upon the existence of the deal between Imageview and Dundee. It was the secrecy of the transaction that fell foul of an agent's fiduciary duty to his client. It appears that the courts, at least until 2019, will be charged with the primary responsibility for monitoring the conduct of football agents in particular, in light of FIFA's decision in 2015 to discontinue its formal regulation of agents. However, FIFA appears poised to re-introduce agent regulation some time in 2019.[232] This is a welcome move but will still probably garner a mixed response, with support from football regulators and governing bodies and resistance from the agents themselves.

230. [2009] EWCA Civ 63.
231. *Ibid.*, at para. 6.
232. 'FIFA agrees to limit loan deals and re-introduce agent regulation'-www.bbc.com/sport, 25 Sep. 2018.

§5. EMPLOYMENT LAW: OTHER SPORTS

346. The landscape with regard to employment law's impact on other sport personalities in Trinidad and Tobago, predictably, is an evolving one. By virtue of their selection to represent the regional cricket team-the Windies[233]-some of Trinidad and Tobago's cricketers have felt the direct impact of labour law through the legal interpretation of successive CBAs. This process has, at times, led to acrimony between players and CWI as summarised in the media at the end of 2014:

> On September 19, 2014, following years of often bitter disputes, the WICB and the West Indies Players Association (WIPA) signed a new collective bargaining agreement and memorandum of understanding. The agreement, according to WIPA, was expected to bring 'stability' to the system, but on the eve of West Indies' first One-Day International (ODI) on a tour to India, one-day captain Dwayne Bravo came out strongly against WIPA president Wavell Hinds, claiming that he had 'hoodwinked' the team by signing an agreement that resulted in a significant pay-cut for the players.[234]

347. Dwayne Bravo, a cricketer from Santa Cruz, Trinidad,[235] has distinguished himself as a world-class T/20 cricketer, having signed many lucrative contracts to participate in worldwide leagues such as the Indian Premier League, the Caribbean Premier League (CPL) and Australia's Big Bash. Back in 2014, he was the captain of the West Indies ODI team as it played a five-match series in India. The tour had a disastrous end.

348. The Windies team refused to play the fourth ODI and the balance of the tour of India was aborted. The BCCI suggested an initial damages claim of about USD 65 million as a result of the cancelled tour, which had matches still outstanding in all three formats of the game.[236] The claim, eventually stated at USD 42 million, was based, *inter alia*, on loss of income that would have accrued particularly through broadcast rights, sponsorship deals and advertising revenue.

349. From a cricketing perspective, bilateral relations were immediately suspended but eventually lifted in December 2015 on the condition, among others, that the abandoned tour would be completed. The West Indies went on to host India between July and August 2016.

350. Since that fateful tour of India, Bravo has not been selected to represent the Windies and neither has fellow Trinidadian Kieron Pollard, the hard-hitting T/20 global star. It is believed that CWI saw Pollard as playing a very supportive role to

233. Formerly known as 'West Indies'
234. ESPNCricinfo Staff, *Full Coverage of the West Indies Payment Dispute*, http://www.espncricinfo.com/story/_/id/21299252/full-coverage-west-indies-payment-dispute.
235. Coincidentally, Santa Cruz is also the village from which cricket legend Brian Lara originates.
236. Cricket has three main formats: test cricket which lasts a maximum of five days, 50-over cricket and 20/20 cricket.

Bravo in the lead up to the abortion of the India tour. Yet, notwithstanding what many in the region believe has been payback for Bravo and Pollard for the role in the cancelled tour, the root of the conflicts in India stemmed from a battle between the players and their own union.

351. At the very core of concluding a legally binding contract, is the agreement of the parties or meeting of the minds, the well-known *consensus ad idem*. It is in this very regard that legal complexities took root in 2014 because despite the signing of a CBA and MOU between CWI and the WIPA, the commitment of the latter's President, Wavell Hinds, did not reflect the desires of many of the players, especially the international stars, including Trinidad and Tobago players like Bravo, his younger brother Darren Bravo, Pollard, Sunil Narine, Lendl Simmons, Denesh Ramdin, Ravi Rampaul and Samuel Badree. No one could have foreseen the magnitude of these events and the fallout legally, contractually and relationally.

352. Previous CBAs between CWI and the WIPA have outlined goals including the promotion and maintenance of harmonious industrial relations, the promotion of orderly collective bargaining processes and fostering an environment that is conducive to the effective resolution of disputes.[237] These objectives represent the spirit of good industrial relations practice, both within and outside of the sports sector. By way of comparison, the Professional Cricketing Partnership that exists between New Zealand Cricket (NZC) and the Cricket Players Association (CPA) admirably echoes this conciliatory approach.

353. The Partnership, which functions within the broader framework of a Master Agreement between the NZC, CPA and the Cricket Associations of Otago, Canterbury, Auckland, Wellington and the Northern and Central Districts of New Zealand, identifies the following vision: 'To deliver a professional cricket environment in New Zealand which produces world class players and teams that succeed on the international stage.'[238] This is all occurring in a context where the stakeholders have indicated that they 'recognise the role played by each other party in the operation of the business of Professional Cricket in New Zealand, and agree that this is necessarily founded upon a relationship of partnership between them'.[239] Unfortunately, the West Indian context has not been as harmonious.

354. The well-documented history of conflicts has had a spin-off at many levels, reaching as high as Heads of Government within CARICOM. Each of the key relationships will be explored briefly below.

237. Template CBA between the WICB and the WIPA ending in 2008.
238. New Zealand Cricket Master Agreement at para. 1.10.
239. *Ibid.*, at para. 1.9.

I. The Players and the WIPA

355. The following excerpt helps to offer some context to the labour law impasse that mushroomed from the aborted 2014 tour of India:

> In a jolt to the West Indies players, the WICB has made it clear to them that it will 'engage' only with the West Indies Players Association (WIPA) in any attempt to break the deadlock between the groups. Dave Cameron, the WICB president stated … that the board was willing to play a mediating role, but strictly under the new guidelines laid out in the Memorandum of Understanding (MoU) signed between the WICB and the WIPA in September.[240]

356. As far as Cameron was concerned, the then-WICB would only recognise the WIPA as the bona fide entity through whom possible mediation would occur subsequent to the 2014 India debacle. The message was conveyed pellucidly that the WICB saw itself as having a legal relationship with the WIPA via the CBA and MOU, and that any discussions would be strictly on those terms. Fast forward to the March 2016 pre-World Cup[241] contract dispute and skipper Sammy said that his players wanted to speak face to face and not through the WIPA.

357. The strength of Cameron's position comes from the fact that previous CBAs explicitly stated that the WIPA was the exclusive representative and bargaining agent for players selected on the West Indies team. For Sammy and his charges to have any *locus standi* in initiating settlement talks, it would appear that some form of individual match contracts would have needed to be in place, perhaps with Dispute Resolution clauses facilitating good faith negotiations.

358. Here is where the players are caught and bowled! Typically, match tour or retainer contracts for the players are incorporated into the CBA and MOU and form a part of the prevailing terms and conditions. The individual contract, therefore, does not exist as a stand-alone document but gets its real legal weight from being a part of the CBA. Outside of WIPA membership, the players risk remaining exposed to being left out of the legal and financial benefits intended for Windies cricketers.

II. The WIPA and the WICB

359. In the Caribbean, the Patterson Report[242] is well known. It, too, offers further context to the history of employment-based disputes in regional cricket:

---

240. Nagraj Gollapudi, *WICB Ready to Mediate But Will Only Talk to WIPA*, ESPNCricinfo, http://www.espncricinfo.com/westindies/content/story/789697.html, 16 Oct. 2014.
241. The ICC T/20 Cricket World Cup 2016 was played in India.
242. P.J. Patterson et al., Committee on Governance of West Indies Cricket-Final Report, 2007.

> A most unfortunate occurrence, especially in the recent past, is the tense and fractious relationships that have developed between the WICB and the players who are represented by WIPA. Differences have largely centred on the question of remuneration of the players, but neither side has demonstrated a sufficient flexibility and disposition to settle industrial claims through the regular modalities of bargaining. Far too often, the settlement has to depend on arbitration, which is a costly and time-consuming method for settlement.[243]

360. The Patterson Report is a significant document within West Indian circles. It stands out among various written summaries and analyses of cricket in the Caribbean, having been spearheaded by former Jamaican Prime Minister Percival J. Patterson. Indeed, the word 'fractious' best described the nature of the relationship between the WICB and the WIPA for many years, with commercial considerations often planting seeds of division between these two major stakeholders.

361. It is somewhat ironic, though, that such discord has existed in view of the values articulated in a former strategic plan (for the period 2008–2012), including the creation of 'an organization which adheres to, and upholds, the values of fairness, transparency, equity, equality and respect for all involved in the game, especially the players'. Notably, the strategic plan was revised in 2011 and earmarked to run until 2016. Among the goals articulated in the latter document was improving the relationship with the WIPA, adding that 'WIPA is critical to the achievement of WICB's Strategic Direction'.[244]

362. Although there has been a welcome improvement in their relationship over the past few years, the general tone of their shaky partnership is captured well in a case decided in the High Court of Trinidad and Tobago, *West Indies Cricket Board Inc v. West Indies Players' Association.*[245] Justice Andre Des Vignes repeated the salient submissions of the WIPA who, as Defendant, held the view that the WICB 'frustrated the intent and purpose of the CBA'. The WIPA further alleged that 'as a consequence, they have endured both pecuniary and non-pecuniary losses including inability to fulfil its obligations to its members in negotiating for appropriate terms and conditions'.[246]

363. It is noteworthy from the WIPA's assertions that, at that time, it saw the WICB's actions as hampering its ability to represent its members effectively in contract negotiations. In 2016, the international players, apparently, did not desire representation from the WIPA. That is a problem that essentially remained outside of the reach of the WICB.

243. *Ibid.*
244. WICB Strategic Plan 2011–2016, at p. 45.
245. CV 2012-00046.
246. Paragraph 19.

III. The WICB and CARICOM

364. In what may be considered an anomaly in sports governance, given the emphasis placed on the autonomy of National and International Governing Bodies, CARICOM has in place a Prime Ministerial Sub-Committee on the Governance of West Indies Cricket. The very name of the body suggests that regional political leaders have a direct impact on the governance of a sport that has a heritage and tradition that transcends the boundary lines.

365. However, a group called Cricket Legends in a press release of April 2016 did not hesitate to highlight that although 'the WICB might see itself as a private entity, it is there for a public good and should therefore be accountable, in some way, to the governments and people of the Caribbean'.[247] They added further that in 2015, 'the Supreme Court of India[248] made that very point to the privately run Board of Control for Cricket in India'.[249]

366. There is growing traction, at least within cricket, therefore, that the public interest element may be a factor that is sufficiently weighty to justify the involvement of Governments, if there is a real and legitimate concern that those in charge are not managing sport in the best interests of the wider society. Herein lies the sometimes illusive and often controversial distinction between government involvement and government interference. The former is deemed essential, opportune and welcome. By contrast, the latter is interpreted as inimical to sporting autonomy and is often met with threats of suspension.

§6. Employment Law and Sports Administrators

367. Most of the sports-based employment cases that have been ventilated in Trinidad and Tobago have been heard before the country's Industrial Court and involved claims of unfair dismissal from the SPORTT. Many past and present SPORTT employees have had significant experience in sports administration, making them valuable resources.

368. Yet, a number of former employees have not hesitated to commence legal action against SPORTT through their respective representative unions. In *Banking Insurance and General Workers Union v. The Sport Company of Trinidad and Tobago*,[250] the Industrial Court upheld the claim of former sports administrator, Charles Branche, that he was wrongfully dismissed and that the actions of SPORTT were in breach of good and proper industrial relations practice. The following sections of the Industrial Relations Act Chapter 88:01 were considered:

247. *Ibid.*
248. This was a reference to the previously mentioned decision in Board of Control for Cricket in *India v. Cricket Association of Bihar*, Civil Appeal No. 4235 of 2014. *See* n. 120.
249. *Ibid.*
250. TT 2014 IC 52.

> 10(4) Notwithstanding any rule of law to the contrary, but subject to subsections (5) and (6), in addition to its jurisdiction and powers under this Part, the Court may, in any dispute concerning the dismissal of a worker, order the re-employment or reinstatement (in his former or a similar position) of any worker, subject to such conditions as the Court thinks fit to impose, or the payment of compensation or damages whether or not in lieu of such reemployment or reinstatement, or the payment of exemplary damages [i]n lieu of such reemployment or reinstatement
>
> (5) An order under subsection (4) may be made where, in the opinion of the Court, a worker has been dismissed [i]n circumstances that are harsh and oppressive or not in accordance with the principles of good industrial relations practice; and [i]n the case of an order for compensation or damages, the Court [i]n making an assessment thereon shall not be bound to follow any rule of law for the assessment of compensation or damages and the Court may make an assessment that is in its opinion fair and appropriate.[251]

369. In ruling in favour of the employee, the Industrial Court noted, *inter alia*, his experience as a sports administrator, having served the Governments of both the Cayman Islands and Trinidad and Tobago. It held that the worker was dismissed in breach of his employment contract awarding him approximately USD 90,000 in damages plus exemplary damages in the sum of about USD 30,000.

370. There was a similar outcome in *Communication Workers Union v. The Sports Company of Trinidad and Tobago*[252] where the employee, Mr Selwyn Singh, was awarded approximately USD 13000.00 inclusive of exemplary damages in circumstances where SPORTT itself, as employer, was candid enough to concede that the worker's dismissal was harsh and oppressive and contrary to the principles of good industrial relations practice.[253]

371. In *National Union of Government and Federated Workers v. The Sport Company of Trinidad and Tobago*,[254] there was uncontroverted evidence from the dismissed worker that her contract was terminated prematurely, unilaterally and unlawfully. In examining the applicable legal principles, the Court accepted the general rule that at common law, a worker is entitled to compensation for the unexpired period of his or her contract subject to his or her duty to mitigate loss.[255] Again, the Court used its powers under section 10 of the Industrial Relations Act to award the employee, Mrs. Aisha Kalloo, damages in the sum of approximately USD 58,000.

251. *Ibid.*, paras 4–5.
252. TT 2012 IC 80.
253. *Ibid.* The Industrial Court, on similar legal grounds, also ruled in favour of multiple employees in *Communications Workers Union v. SPORTT* [TT 2014 IC 49] and *Communications Workers Union v SPORTT [TT 2012] IC 82.*
254. TT 2013 IC 66.
255. *Ibid.*, paras 5–6.

372. The general picture to be painted, however, is that outside of the litigation involving SPORTT as employer, there is an overall absence of employment-related case law in the local sports sector.

§7. CONCLUSION

373. The contract of employment has evolved. The Industrial Court in the 2014 decision of *National Union of Government and Federated Workers v. The Sport Company of Trinidad and Tobago*[256] noted as much when it cited from the House of Lords ruling in *Johnson v. Unisys Limited*[257] as follows:

> At common law the contract of employment was regarded by the courts as a contract like any other. The parties were free to negotiate whatever terms they liked and no terms would be implied unless they satisfied the strict test of necessity applied to a commercial contract. Freedom of contract meant that the stronger party, usually the employer, was free to impose his terms upon the weaker. But over the last 30 years or so, the nature of the contract of employment has been transformed. It has been recognized that a person's employment is usually one of the most important things in his or her life, it gives not only a livelihood but an occupation, an identity and a sense of self-esteem. The law has changed to recogniz[e] this social reality.[258]

The Industrial Court added that the employment contract has an identity of its own.[259]

374. The trend in Trinidad and Tobago has been that there is typically greater sympathy for the employee than the employer. Yet, this tends to be in the context of trade disputes that have been heard and determined in the Industrial Court. The dearth of case law in Trinidad and Tobago as it relates to sportspersons in their contracts of employment leaves this area of sports law largely underdeveloped. This is likely to remain the case until the value of sports-related employment in the country is augmented significantly.

256. TT 2014 IC 47.
257. [2001] IRLR 279.
258. *Ibid.*
259. *Ibid.*

Part III. Doping and Sport

Chapter 1. General Issues

375. For a long time, doping in sport has been considered to be one of the biggest threats to the integrity of sport rivalled, perhaps, only by match-fixing. The use of performance-enhancing substances goes against the spirit of sport and the attendant principles of ethics, honesty, sportsmanship and fair play that have become so central to the practice of sport. The 2015 World Anti-Doping Code (WADC) ('the Code') describes doping as fundamentally contrary to the spirit of sport, which itself is defined as the celebration of the human spirit, body and mind.[260]

376. After the successful drafting and adoption of the 2003, 2009 and 2015 Codes, significant progress has already been made in the formulation of the 2021 Code. On 10 December 2018, the World Anti-Doping Agency (WADA) launched the third phase of its global consultation process as feedback was solicited from stakeholders from all over the world, representing both public authorities and the sports movement.

377. The Code outlines its own objectives by stating that its purpose is 'to advance the anti-doping effort through universal harmonization of core anti-doping elements'.[261] It adds that the Code 'is intended to be specific enough to achieve complete harmonization on issues where uniformity is required, yet general enough in other areas to permit flexibility on how agreed-upon anti-doping principles are implemented'.[262]

378. These are commendable goals which continue to be refined as anti-doping organisations seek to establish the balance between legal and regulatory certainty and predictability on the one hand, and proportionality on the other hand. Indeed, the drafters of the Code have been compelled to keep in view the need to respect the human and fundamental rights of sports participants.

260. Page 14.
261. Page 11.
262. *Ibid.*

379. Soek's[263] thought-provoking questions, in the context of the controversial whereabouts provisions, captured the essence of the above-mentioned balancing act. He noted:

> The possibility of disturbing a sportsperson in his private life and home to take a doping sample, gives rise to a number of interesting questions … The first issue which arises is the legal basis of such checks performed outside a competition context, and the status of the legal basis. If the basis resides in 'purely sportive rules', does the court then have the possibility to test the rules? Can it be taken as a point of departure that no single objective of the sporting sector can justify that the more fundamental social interests and rights of the sportsperson are violated? In other words: are the interests of the sporting world only related to the autonomous private rights, or are these interests subordinate to the rules of the human rights treaties? If the answer to this is that the sporting world must step aside for fundamental human rights, the follow-up question must be whether the right the sporting world accords itself to carry out doping checks at the home of a sportsperson or during his or her holiday, is in conflict with basic rights. Finally, there is the question as to whether in choosing to exercise a sport, the sportsperson has voluntarily renounced the protection human rights offers.[264]

380. These are difficult questions with no simple answers. Their complexity causes them to be ventilated regularly before human rights courts, national courts and arbitral tribunals. Recently, in *National Federation of Sportspersons' Associations and Unions (FNASS) and others v. France*,[265] the European Court of Human Rights addressed the question of whether anti-doping regulations breached the human rights of athletes.

381. The applicants in this case asserted that the whereabouts requirement, in particular, stood in breach of Article 8 of the European Convention on Human Rights (ECHR). The oft-cited Article 8 states that:

(1) Everyone has the right to respect for his private and family life, his home and his correspondence.
(2) There shall be no interference by a public authority with the exercise of this right except such as is in accordance with the law and is necessary in a democratic society in the interests of national security, public safety or the economic well-being of the country, for the prevention of disorder or crime, for the protection of health or morals, or for the protection of the rights and freedoms of others.

---

263. Janwillem Soek, *The Athlete's Right to Respect for His Private Life and His Home* 3–4 Int. Sports Law J., 3 (2008).
264. *Ibid.*
265. Applications nos. 48151/11 and 77769/13, decision dated 18 Jan. 2018 and revised on 18 Apr. 2018.

382. The Court's articulation of the prevailing legal principles was instructive. It noted in paragraphs 152–154, in part, as follows:

> The Court reiterates that the concepts of private and family life are broad terms not susceptible to exhaustive definition … The concept of 'family life' implies that those concerned are allowed to lead a normal family life) … The concept of 'private life' is initially understood as the right to privacy, that is, the right to live, as far as one wishes, protected from publicity … or the right to live privately, away from unwanted attention.
>
> Article 8 protects the right to personal development, whether in terms of personality or of personal autonomy, which is an important principle underlying the interpretation of the Article 8 guarantees … It encompasses the right for each individual to approach others in order to establish and develop relationships with them and with the outside world, that is, the right to a 'private social life', and may include professional activities or activities taking place in a public context (*ibid.*, §§ 70 and 71). According to the Court, '[t]here is, therefore, a zone of interaction of a person with others, even in a public context, which may fall within the scope of "private life"'.
>
> The Court further reiterates that, just like 'private life', the concept of 'home' in Article 8 of the Convention is an autonomous concept which does not depend on classification under domestic law but is defined by reference to the factual circumstances, namely the existence of sufficient and continuous links with a specific place … A home will usually be the place, the physically defined area, where private and family life develops. The individual has a right to respect for his home, meaning not just the right to the actual physical area, but also to the quiet enjoyment of that area … Lastly, the concept of home is not confined to places of residence where private life is conducted. It encompasses professional premises, because to interpret the words 'private life' and 'home' as including certain professional or business activities or premises is consonant with the essential object and purpose of Article 8, namely to protect the individual against arbitrary interference by the public authorities.

383. In other words, as the court defined 'family life' 'private life' 'private social life' and 'home' it established an underlying premise that individuals, including sports persons, should receive the law's protection against capricious or arbitrary interference by public authorities.

384. Nevertheless, on the facts of this case the court concluded by stating:

> The Court does not underestimate the impact of the whereabouts requirements on the applicants' private lives. Nevertheless, the general-interest considerations that make them necessary are particularly important and, in the Court's view, justify the restrictions on the applicants' rights under Article 8 of the Convention. Reducing or removing the requirements of which the applicants complain would be liable to increase the dangers of doping to their health and that of the entire sporting community, and would run counter to the European

and international consensus on the need for unannounced testing. The Court therefore finds that the respondent State struck a fair balance between the different interests at stake and that there has been no violation of Article 8 of the Convention.[266]

385. The court's finding in *FNASS v. France* is a reminder that there are competing interests that must be considered and weighed in the fight for clean sport. Public interest factors tend to carry great significance in this equation as seen in *France*. This scenario tends to be replicated on the international scale as various Signatories to the UNESCO Convention seek to implement the applicable provisions.

386. In Trinidad and Tobago, the legislative drafters of the 2013 Anti-Doping in Sport Act (the TT Anti-Doping Act) were conscious of the various rights at stake, including an awareness of the invasive nature of sample collection. In this regard, the TT Anti-Doping Act required a special Parliamentary majority, a reality manifested in the wording of section 3 which stated that the Act shall have effect although it was inconsistent with sections 4 and 5 of the Constitution of Trinidad and Tobago.

387. This and other salient provisions of the TT Anti-Doping Act will be assessed in Chapter 2.

§1. The 2021 World Anti-doping Code: The Review Process

388. As mentioned above, at the time of writing the third phase of the consultation process for the drafting and adoption of the 2021 Code and the related International Standards was already underway. Among the salient recommendations made at the time were:

(1) the addition of an eleventh anti-doping rule violation (ADRV) under the name: Acts by an athlete or other person to discourage or retaliate against reporting;
(2) the re-introduction of the Aggravating Circumstances provision which existed in the 2009 Code but was removed in the 2015 Code;
(3) the addition of two new International Standards, namely, the International Standard for Results Management and the International Standard for Education (ISE); and
(4) the drafting of the Anti-Doping Charter of Athlete Rights.

389. It is anticipated that the final draft of the 2021 Code will be another commendable forward step in the global fight for clean and fair sport.

266. *Ibid.*, para. 191.

Chapter 2. The 2013 Anti-doping in Sport Act: Application and Implementation

390. The TT Anti-Doping Act was passed in the year 2013 and received final Presidential assent on 1 June 2015. It was the fourth such piece of legislation in the Caribbean following the passage of the similarly named Acts in Jamaica in 2008 and 2014, the Bahamas in 2009 and Bermuda in 2011.

391. The long title to the Act states that it is an:

> Act to provide for the implementation of the UNESCO International Convention against Doping in Sport, the establishment of the Trinidad and Tobago Anti-Doping Organisation, the Trinidad and Tobago Anti-Doping Disciplinary Panel and the Trinidad and Tobago Anti-Doping Appeal Panel, the promotion of an anti-doping environment which encourages positive behaviour among participants in sport and dissuades them from using prohibited substances and prohibited methods and for other related matters.

392. As indicated in the foregoing long title, then, the TT Anti-Doping Act seeks to implement the 2005 UNESCO Anti-Doping Convention in Trinidad and Tobago. Additionally, the Act establishes the local NADO to be known as the TTADO.

393. The work of the TTADO itself is to be supported by four other entities in the local regulatory structure:

(1) the Trinidad and Tobago Anti-Doping Disciplinary Panel;
(2) the Trinidad and Tobago Anti-Doping Appeal Panel;
(3) the Results Management Committee; and
(4) the Therapeutic Use Exemption Committee.

394. At the time of writing, none of the foregoing panels or committees were populated.

§1. THE SPECIAL PARLIAMENTARY MAJORITY

395. In Chapter 1, it was mentioned that a special parliamentary majority[267] was needed for this legislation to be passed as a result of the Act's inconsistency with sections 4 and 5 of the Constitution. Section 4 of the Constitution of Trinidad and Tobago provides as follows:

267. A two-thirds majority in both Houses of Parliament, namely, the House of Representatives (Lower House) and the Senate (Upper House).

It is hereby recognised and declared that in Trinidad and Tobago there have existed and shall continue to exist, without discrimination by reason of race, origin, colour, religion or sex, the following fundamental human rights and freedoms, namely:

(a) the right of the individual to life, liberty, security of the person and enjoyment of property and the right not to be deprived thereof except by due process of law;
(b) the right of the individual to equality before the law and the protection of the law;
(c) *the right of the individual to respect for his private and family life*;
(d) the right of the individual to equality of treatment from any public authority in the exercise of any functions;
(e) the right to join political parties and to express political views;
(f) the right of a parent or guardian to provide a school of his own choice for the education of his child or ward;
(g) freedom of movement;
(h) freedom of conscience and religious belief and observance;
(i) freedom of thought and expression;
(j) freedom of association and assembly; and
(k) freedom of the press. [Emphasis added]

396. The above represents the fundamental rights and freedoms to which all citizens of Trinidad and Tobago are entitled. Section 4(c) uses language that is similar to Article 8 of the ECHR.

397. Section 5(1) of the Constitution lays out the parameters for the protection of the section 4 rights by stating that, outside of certain express exceptions, 'no law may abrogate, abridge or infringe or authorise the abrogation, abridgment or infringement of any of the rights and freedoms hereinbefore recognised and declared'. It is because of the language of section 5(1) that the TT Anti-Doping Act could be deemed inconsistent with the constitution since the doping statute is a law that infringes on an individual's respect for his private life.[268]

§2. The Scope of the Act

398. Section 5 of the Act identifies the scope of its application. The following categories of persons are captured by the legislation:

(1) athletes who are:
 (a) citizens or residents of Trinidad and Tobago;
 (b) in or outside of Trinidad and Tobago; and

268. *See FNASS v. France*, *supra*, n. 265 for the court's definition of 'private life'.

(c) in-competition or out-of-competition;
(2) athlete support personnel who are citizens or residents of Trinidad and Tobago when they are in Trinidad and Tobago or when they are outside of Trinidad and Tobago for the purpose of supporting an athlete;
(3) athletes who are not citizens or residents of Trinidad and Tobago when they are training or competing in Trinidad and Tobago;
(4) athlete support personnel who are not citizens or residents of Trinidad and Tobago when they are in Trinidad and Tobago for the purpose of supporting an athlete;
(5) national governing bodies and their affiliate members, clubs, teams, associations or leagues; and
(6) sporting organisations not affiliated with an NGB.

399. The legislation, therefore, captures a fairly broad base of persons, starting with athletes and their support personnel. An 'athlete' is defined as 'a person who participates in a sport as (a) an international-level athlete; (b) a national-level athlete; or (c) any other competitor in sport who is otherwise subject to the jurisdiction of a signatory to the Code or any other sports organisation accepting the Code'.[269] The intent here, then, was to capture competitive athletes and not those participating recreationally.

400. The term 'athlete support personnel' also has a thorough definition in the TT Anti-Doping Act. This group refers to:

(1) a parent or guardian of an athlete who is a minor;
(2) a medical practitioner or paramedical personnel, including a psychiatrist and a psychologist;
(3) a coach, trainer, manager, official, agent or team staff; or
(4) any other person, working with or treating or assisting an athlete participating in or preparing for sports competition, including a physiotherapist and a nutritionist.[270]

401. The intent, in this regard, is captured in the last category of persons, which is to place under the cloak of legislative regulation all those persons who help an athlete that is either participating in or is preparing to participate in a sports competition. The preparation is not limited to physical preparation which would embrace persons like doctors, trainers, coaches and nutritionists but also includes mental and psychological preparation so that psychiatrists and psychologists are also included.

402. It is to be noted that the athletes and the support personnel in view are not only citizens of Trinidad and Tobago but also residents, so that non-nationals of the country are also contemplated by the legislation. Additionally, sporting bodies that

269. Anti-Doping in Sport Act, Ch. 40:56, s. 4.
270. *Ibid.*

are involved in formal sport are also caught by the *TT Anti-Doping Act*, so that National Governing Bodies and their member clubs and affiliates are all subject to the legislation.

§3. The Role and Functions of the TTADO

403. The TTADO is established as a body corporate pursuant to section 7(1) of the TT Anti-Doping Act. The TTADO's mandate is found in both the 2015 Code and the legislation. The legislative functions include the following:

(1) planning, implementing and directing a National Anti-Doping Programme aimed at informing or educating athletes, athlete support personnel, parents, the media and the general public in Trinidad and Tobago about antidoping matters, including:
  (a) the health consequences of doping, including the use of anabolic steroids in fitness centres;
  (b) the harm of doping to the ethical values of sport;
  (c) prohibited substances and prohibited methods;
  (d) therapeutic use exemptions;
  (e) nutritional supplements;
  (f) doping control procedures; and
  (g) the rights and responsibilities of athletes and the consequences of committing an ADRV;
(2) facilitating the sharing of information among national governing bodies, sporting organisations and other relevant agencies to reduce the prevalence and availability of prohibited substances and methods;
(3) facilitating the access of national governing bodies to laboratories accredited by WADA for doping control analysis;
(4) entering into reciprocal testing agreements with NADOs outside Trinidad and Tobago;
(5) consulting with, advising and assisting Government departments and agencies, local authorities, the TTOC, national governing bodies, sporting organisations and other bodies and persons on anti-doping matters;
(6) advising the Minister on anti-doping matters;
(7) making recommendations pursuant to section 37;[271]
(8) initiating and supporting rehabilitation programmes for athletes who have used prohibited substances;
(9) performing such other functions as are necessary to implement or facilitate effective anti-doping measures.[272]

271. Section 37 states as follows: 'Where a national governing body does not comply with the provisions of this Act, TTADO may make recommendations to the Minister to withhold, in whole or in part, financial or nonfinancial support from the national governing body.'
272. Section 7(2).

404. These functions closely mirror the roles and responsibilities of NADOs outlined in Article 20.5 of the 2015 Code. The 2021 draft Code proposes to add new responsibilities which are not found in the 2015 Code. Some of the key proposals for addition to the Code include the following:

(1) While NADOs are still expected to be independent in the operational decisions and activities, the 2021 draft Code specifies what those activities could include, for instance, the adoption and enforcement of a conflict of interest policy which prohibits any involvement by its directors and officers in the management of any International Federation, National Federation, NOC or Major Event Organisation.[273]
(2) NADOs are now being called to plan, implement and evaluate anti-doping education in line with the requirements of the new ISE.[274]
(3) NADOs must now require all of their directors, officers, employees and volunteers to agree to and be bound by anti-doping rules in accordance with the Code as a condition of their position or involvement with the NADO.[275]
(4) Significantly, NADOs are also being mandated to respect the operational independence of laboratories as provided in the International Standard for Laboratories.[276]

§4. Operational Elements of the TT Anti-doping Act

405. The practical functioning of the TTADO includes the establishment of a Registered Testing Pool (RTP), in which the TTADO must also publish the criteria for the inclusion of an athlete's name in the RTP.[277] A Results Management Committee[278] and a Therapeutic Use Exemption (TUE) Committee[279] are also established with clear responsibilities that will accord with WADA's International Standards, especially the International Standard for TUEs.

§5. The Whereabouts Requirements

406. Section 23 of the TT Anti-Doping Act provides for the controversial whereabouts requirements. That section states:

(1) A national-level athlete and an international-level athlete in the RTP of TTADO shall, before the beginning of each quarter, submit to TTADO on such form as TTADO may approve, a quarterly whereabouts filing that provides

273. 2021 Draft Code dated 10 Dec. 2018, Art. 20.5.1.
274. *Ibid.*, Art. 20.5.8.
275. *Ibid.*, Art. 20.5.10.
276. *Ibid.*, Art. 20.5.14.
277. Anti-Doping in Sport Act, Ch. 40:56, s. 16.
278. *Ibid.*, s. 19.
279. *Ibid.*, s. 17.

accurate and complete information about the whereabouts of the athlete during that quarter, including information specifying:
(a) where he will, on a daily basis, be living, training and competing during that quarter so that he can be located for testing at any time during that quarter; and
(b) for each day in that quarter, one hour when he will be available at a specified location for testing.

(2) Where any change in circumstances requires the updating of information in the quarterly whereabouts filing of an athlete, the athlete shall update the information as soon as possible and in any event prior to the next one-hour period specified in the filing under subsection (1)(b).

(3) Where an athlete is required to provide whereabouts information to an International Federation, he shall simultaneously provide a copy of the information to TTADO.

(4) Subject to the Anti-Doping Rules, an athlete who does not comply with subsection (1) or (2) shall be:
(a) ineligible for financial or other support from the Government upon recommendation from TTADO;
(b) prohibited from participating in national and international competitions as may be provided in the Anti-Doping Rules; and
(c) such other sanctions as may be provided for in the Anti-Doping Rules.

407. The provisions of section 23 above mirror the stipulations of the International Standard for Testing and Investigations[280] as well as Article 2.4 of the 2015 Code. It is important to note that the whereabouts requirements are restricted to athletes who are in the RTP. The effect of this stipulation is that only a small number of athletes will actually be subject to these provisions.

408. 'RTP' has been defined in the TT Anti-Doping Act as 'the pool established by each International Federation and National Anti-Doping Organisation of international-level athletes who are subject to both in-competition and out-of-competition testing as part of that International Federation's or National Anti-Doping Organisation's test distribution plan'. Herein lies one of the aspects of the statute that should be proposed for amendment. While section 23 refers to both national and international-level athletes being in the RTP of the TTADO, the definition of RTP in section 4 is limited only to international-level athletes. The statutory inconsistency, then, ought to be remedied to bring harmony between these two provisions.

409. Guidance can be found in this regard by referring to the definition of RTP in the 2015 Code, where it is defined as the 'pool of highest-priority Athletes established separately at the international level by International Federations and at the national level by National Anti-Doping Organizations, who are subject to focused

280. Article 4.8 and Annex I, 2017 edition.

In-Competition and Out-of-Competition Testing as part of that International Federation's or National Anti-Doping Organization's test distribution plan and therefore are required to provide whereabouts information as provided in Article 5.6 and the International Standard for Testing and Investigations'. Notably, the Code contemplates both national-level and international-level athletes with the emphasis being placed on athletes of the 'highest priority'. While no comment is given in the Code to explain what is meant by 'highest-priority athletes', at face value, it seems reasonable to interpret that expression to mean athletes either at the peak of their respective sports and who the relevant anti-doping organisation deems it necessary to target, perhaps due to dramatic rise in sports performance.

410. As mentioned earlier in Chapter 1, the European Court of Human Rights in the *FNASS* case recently ruled that the whereabouts provisions strike the right balance between doping control and respect for the rights of athletes. No cases have yet been litigated in Trinidad and Tobago with regard to the whereabouts requirements. Were such a situation to arise, the likely defendant would be the NGB with conduct of the doping control process or the TTOC, which currently stands as the de facto NADO[281] until the TTADO Board is appointed and its supporting committees established.

411. Still, the practical operation of the whereabouts rule continues to be contentious especially with respect to issue of the protection of fundamental rights. Soek's analysis captured the dilemma quite well when he observed that a:

> [G]overnment has the responsibility to ensure that individuals can enjoy their fundamental rights in practice. Measures can be expected from a government, should the rights of one individual be harmed by another individual. The Code has created a situation in which a private law organisation (the WADA or a national anti-doping organisation) is enabled to violate the rights of an individual (a sportsperson). Checking the doping use of a sportsperson who is enjoying his or her leisure time in a home environment, on holiday with his family or in his office, cannot be seen in any other way than a violation of his right to 'respect for his private and family life and his home.' In signing the Copenhagen Declaration and ratifying the UNESCO Convention, the countries which are party to the ECHR[282] and which had on its basis a 'positive obligation' to guarantee the fundamental rights of a sportsperson, have grouped behind the WADA mission and have accepted the principles of the Code.[283]

412. While the European Court of Human Rights in *FNASS* has not lamented the application of the whereabouts rules in the same manner as Soek, this may not be the final word on this issue. The courts in Trinidad and Tobago have been put on notice in anticipation of possible future doping litigation when the local legislation

281. Article 20.4.6, 2015 WADC.
282. ECHR.
283. Soek, *supra*, n. 263, at 8.

is fully operationalised. Indeed, the TTADO has been charged with the responsibility of advising the Minister with responsibility for sport, on anti-doping matters and this is likely to encompass the offering of legal opinions as to how the global regulatory community has managed threats of litigation in the face of their anti-doping rules and regulations.

§6. The Disciplinary and Appeals Panels

413. There are two main adjudicatory panels under the TTADO's legislative structure, namely, the Disciplinary Panel[284] and the Appeal Panel[285] Such is their prominence that their respective members are appointed by the Head of State, the President of the Republic of Trinidad and Tobago.[286]

414. The Disciplinary Panel has as its main functions the following activities:

(1) to receive written references from the Results Management Committee alleging the commission of an ADRV;
(2) to receive and examine evidence relating to alleged ADRVs;
(3) to conduct disciplinary hearings relating to alleged ADRVs;
(4) to determine whether an ADRV has been committed;
(5) to impose sanctions for ADRVs.

415. It means, therefore, that once the Results Management Committee has referred an alleged ADRV to the Disciplinary Panel, the latter is now charged with the responsibility of determining if in fact the ADRV has been committed and what sanctions would apply. Those sanctions, found in section 26(3) of the Act include the following:

(1) disqualification from a particular competition or event;
(2) ineligibility for participation in any competition or other activity for a specified period of time;
(3) ineligibility for funding for a specified period of time; or
(4) suspension from participating in any competition prior to the final decision of the Disciplinary Panel.

416. The Disciplinary Panel may enforce one or more of the above sanctions.

417. Pursuant to section 33(1) of the Act, the Appeal Panel shall hear and determine:

(1) appeals from a decision of the Disciplinary Panel:
  (a) that an ADRV was committed;

284. Anti-Doping in Sport Act Ch. 40:56, s. 27.
285. *Ibid.*, s. 31.
286. *Ibid.*, ss 28(1) and 32(1).

   (b) imposing sanctions for an ADRV;
   (c) that no ADRV was committed; or
   (d) that an ADRV proceeding cannot go forward for procedural reasons;
(2) appeals from a decision to impose sanctions referred to in section 26(3);
(3) appeals from a decision of the TUE Committee to grant or refuse a TUE to a national-level athlete;
(4) appeals from a decision of an anti-doping organisation on the grounds that it lacks jurisdiction to rule on an alleged ADRV or on the imposition of sanctions in relation thereto;
(5) appeals from a decision by an anti-doping organisation not to bring forward an Adverse Analytical Finding or an Atypical Finding as an ADRV or a possible ADRV, as the case may be;
(6) appeals from a decision by an anti-doping organisation or other body not to go forward with a possible ADRV after an investigation required under the Anti-Doping Rules; and
(7) appeals from a decision to impose a provisional suspension as a result of a provisional hearing or a decision concerning the violation of a provisional suspension.

418. Again, neither of the foregoing panels has been called into action in Trinidad and Tobago due to the absence of the respective office-holders and members. As a result, the practice in Trinidad and Tobago is for the NGBs to prosecute cases against athletes who have committed an ADRV.

419. In the next chapter, a detailed legal analysis will be done on two high profile cases both from the sport of athletics and both of which reached the CAS for final determination.

§7. Comment: The Criminalisation of Doping Through Legislation

420. In the middle of 2018, the US Senate proposed the introduction of the *Rodchenkov Anti-Doping Act of 2018.*[287] The short title of the Act identified its goal as the establishment of criminal penalties and civil remedies for doping fraud violations at major international competitions. The Act sought to follow the lead of countries such as Germany, Austria, Belgium, Denmark, France, Italy, Sweden, Switzerland and Spain.[288]

421. The Act identified some of the ills that it sought to cure, such as:

(1) the damage caused to the integrity of sport;
(2) the fostering of bribery and money laundering; and
(3) the cheating effect that doping fraud has on clean athletes and also on sponsoring corporations.

---

287. The Act was named after Russian whistleblower Dr. Grigory Rodchenkov.
288. Section 4.

422. The question as to whether the criminalisation of doping is a proportionate response to the threat of doping has produced varying opinions. Sumner[289] addressed the issue noting that 'the current system of anti-doping sanctions are ineffective in efficiently reducing doping and that this results in the public's loss of faith in the performances it sees and the loss of the "spirit of sport"'.[290]

423. Her proposal to criminalise doping has a similar foundation as the drafters of the Rodchenkov Anti-Doping Act. She believes that criminalisation would be based on what she called the fraud model, upon which she elucidated by stating that under 'the fraud model an athlete caught doping would commit a fraud by falsely representing that they were competing clean with the intention to make a financial gain for themselves in the form of prize money or sponsorship'.[291]

424. This matter has not been formally addressed in Trinidad and Tobago. The current Anti-Doping in Sport Act contains no such provision, meaning that it would take legislative amendment to introduce and implement any such statutory intent going forward. The tendency to err on the side of conservatism, though, makes it unlikely that such an amendment will occur in Trinidad and Tobago in the near future.

289. Claire Sumner, *The Spirit of Sport: The Case for Criminalisation of Doping in the UK*, 16 *Int. Sports Law J.*, 217–227 (2017).
290. *Ibid.*, p. 218.
291. *Ibid.*

Chapter 3. Trinidad and Tobago Athletes Before the CAS

425. No country wants to have any type of track record for drug use among its athletes. Unfortunately, Trinidad and Tobago cannot lay claim to being the exception to the rule as it, too, has seen its athletes test positive for prohibited substances. Among those reported to have committed ADRVs in previous years were teenaged sprinter Jamie Payne back in 2007 and 400-metre runner Ato Modibo (a.k.a. Ato Stephens).

426. Within recent years, two international-level athletes committed ADRVs which were eventually appealed all the way to the CAS, where both matters were settled prior to the commencement of the actual hearings. These two cases form the subject matter of this chapter and will be given due attention except for the details of the settlement agreement.

427. Due to the fact that there was no published final award from the CAS, the names of the athletes have not been revealed.[292]

§1. CAS 2013/A/3277

I. The Local Hearing: The Disciplinary Committee of the NAAATT

428. In or around November 2012, the Athlete (hereinafter referred to as 'Athlete 1') was informed that she tested positive for the prohibited substance methylhexaneamine (MHA) while competing for her school in June of that year. As an international-level athlete, she also fell within the disciplinary jurisdiction of the NAAATT, the local NGB for track and field.

429. There are many aspects of this entire case that stood out, not always with good reason. One of those features was the fact that it took five months before Athlete 1 was told about her positive test. Second, it appears that both the NAAATT and the IAAF, as international governing body, only became aware of the positive test by virtue of a media report.

430. The first sanction faced by Athlete 1 was the loss of the championship trophy won by her American university. This punishment would have been imposed by the National Collegiate Athletic Association (NCAA). During the NAAATT disciplinary hearing questions were raised as to whether the NCAA and/or Athlete 1's university should have or actually did communicate directly to the NAAATT to inform it of the positive test. If that had occurred, the NAAATT would itself have informed the IAAF.

292. Both cases were given limited coverage in both the local and international media with the athletes' names being mentioned in those reports.

A. *Athlete 1's Submissions Before the NAAATT Disciplinary Committee*

431. Athlete 1's legal team raised a number of issues from the outset. She submitted that: 'It is a fundamental principle of fairness and law, found in the World Anti-Doping Code and the IAAF Anti-Doping Rules, that a defendant (athlete) should not be found guilty until they have had a chance to challenge the reliability of the evidence against them.' Her lawyers added that: 'In a number of ways, the process … denied [Athlete 1] the opportunity to test and challenge the reliability of the laboratory test results. This denial began when she was not allowed to have an expert witness the B-Sample testing, continued when she was not given the laboratory documents for her sample tests, and culminated when she was not afforded a hearing during which she could voice her challenges to the evidence against her. In summary, [Athlete 1] was not allowed to see the evidence against her, and then, she was not allowed to challenge that evidence. When these two basic and fundamental rights are denied to an athlete, they should not be punished regardless of who did the testing.'[293] Athlete 1, therefore, held the view that her fundamental rights were denied and that in the face of such a denial, she could not face punitive sanctions by any disciplinary body.

432. This was not the only concern raised by her legal team, given that after being informed of her positive test for MHA, as evidenced by the result of the A-Sample analysis, she alleged that she was not allowed to witness the B-Sample analysis, although she was physically present at the US laboratory. What is more, although the B-Sample testing occurred in July of that year, she claimed that it was not until November that she was made aware that the B-Sample was also positive. Her college, with whom she had won the 4 × 100 metre relay title suffered the customary loss of points as well as the championship trophy.

433. Athlete 1 proffered three main arguments in her legal submissions before the NAAATT Disciplinary Panel:

(1) that she was not allowed four fundamental and absolute IAAF testing rights during the course of testing her sample from the NCAA Championship, and therefore the results must be set aside;
(2) the NCAA test results cannot be used pursuant to IAAF Rule 45 because the rule's two pre-conditions have not been satisfied and she was not afforded a hearing to challenge the reliability of the test results; and
(3) all athletes have the right to a full hearing in which the prosecution must prove guilt to a comfortable satisfaction and the athlete can challenge the reliability of the evidence.[294]

434. Each of these arguments will be addressed in turn.

---

293. Legal Brief by Attorneys-at-Law for Athlete 1, at p. 2.
294. *Ibid.*, at p. 4–11.

B. The Fundamental Rights Argument

435. Athlete 1 claimed that any athlete must be notified of the opportunity for him/her or his/her representative to attend the opening and analysis of the B-Sample. This right arose pursuant to Article 37.4 of the *IAAF Competition Rules* for that year as well as Article 7.2 of the 2009 WADC.[295] Article 37.4 states, *inter alia*, that: 'the IAAF Anti-Doping Administrator shall promptly notify the Athlete of … the opportunity for the Athlete and/or his representative to attend the B sample opening procedure and analysis at the scheduled date, time and place, if such analysis is requested'.[296]

436. The language of the IAAF Competition Rules closely mirrors Article 7.2 of the 2009 WADC which states, in part, that: 'the Anti-Doping Organization shall promptly notify the Athlete, in the manner set out in its rules, of … (d) the scheduled date, time and place for the B Sample analysis if the Athlete or Anti-Doping Organization chooses to request an analysis of the B Sample; (e) the opportunity for the Athlete and/or the Athlete's representative to attend the B Sample opening and analysis within the time period specified in the International Standard for Laboratories if such analysis is requested'.

437. In other words, Athlete 1 claimed that she was denied the well-entrenched right to be present at the B-Sample opening analysis and that this omission by the regulatory authorities was sufficient to nullify the finding of an ADRV being committed. She relied on three cases in that regard:

(1) *Wen Tong v. International Judo Federation (IJF)*;[297]
(2) *Kaisa Varis v. International Biathlon Union (IBU)*;[298] *and*
(3) *Tchachina v. International Gymnastics Federation (FIG).*[299]

438. She summarised the learning from these cases, together with the applicable doping regulations in the following manner:

> The World Anti-Doping Code (Articles 7 and 8), the IAAF Competition Rules (Rules 37 and 38), and the CAS precedent of *Tong*, *Varis*, and *Tcha[c]hina* clearly establish that the following procedural steps of the testing process are fundamental and absolute rights, which when not followed, must result, in all cases, in the dismissal of the charges against an athlete:
>
> (1) The athlete must be given the A-Sample laboratory document before attending the B-Sample test (this right allows the athlete or representative, an expert in testing, to knowingly witness the B-Sample opening and testing).

295. At the time of the commission of the alleged ADRV, the 2009 WADC was in force.
296. Article 37.4(f), IAAF Competition Rules 2012–2013.
297. CAS 2010/A/2161.
298. CAS 2008/A/1607.
299. CAS 2002/A/385.

(2) The athlete or a representative of the athlete (an expert in testing procedure) must be allowed to witness the entire B-Sample testing process in the lab (this right allows the representative to fully verify the reliability and correctness of the test results under WADA International Standards for Laboratories).
(3) The athlete must be given the A-Sample and B-Sample laboratory documents (this right allows the athlete to fully verify the reliability and correctness of the test results under WADA International Standards for Laboratories).
(4) The athlete must be allowed to challenge the reliability of the test results at a hearing (this right, to be fully given, necessitates that the athlete be afforded all of the rights listed above).[300]

439. The salient aspect of the *Tong* decision was succinctly stated in paragraphs 9.8 and 9.9 of the ruling, where both *Varis* and *Tchachina*, together with other cases, were cited:

> Moreover, it is now established CAS jurisprudence that the athlete's right to attend the opening and analysis of her B sample is fundamental and, if not respected, the B-sample results must be disregarded. See Tchachina, ¶¶ 22-34 (disregarding B-sample results where neither the athlete nor her federation was given notice of the B-sample analysis). This is so even if denial of that right '*is unlikely to affect the result of a B-sample analysis*'. *Id.*, ¶ 26. This is because an '*athlete's right to be given a reasonable opportunity to observe the opening and testing of a "B" sample is of sufficient importance that it needs to be enforced even in situations where all of the other evidence available indicates that the Appellant committed an anti-doping rule violation.' Varis*, ¶ 123 (disregarding B-sample results where the federation failed to make reasonable efforts to accommodate the athlete's request to have her B sample opened and analyzed in the presence of her representative); *see also Tchachina*, ¶ 29 (explaining that to do otherwise would be to treat the athlete '*as the object of the doping test procedure not its subject*').
>
> This right is '*completely taken away from the athlete when the analysis of the B- sample is conducted without the athlete . . . being given due notification of the relevant date and time.' Tchachina*, ¶ 29. Moreover, it is not possible to remedy such a procedural error through the course of the arbitral process. In contrast to violations of the athlete's right to be heard, the '*arbitration cannot substitute the presence (in its widest definition) of a representative of the athlete at the opening of the B-sample.' Tchachina*, ¶ 33. And where – as here – the rules establish a strict liability regime with respect to doping, *'[i]t is of fundamental importance . . . that the rules have been clearly followed.' (CAS 2003/A/477 Beaton & Scholes v Equestrian Federation of Australian Limited*, ¶ 29, citing CAS 94/129 *USA Shooting & Q. v International Shooting Union*). [Emphasis original]

300. Legal Brief, *supra*, n. 293 at 6.

440. The CAS jurisprudence in this regard, therefore, is clear and consistent. Any omission to afford an athlete the right to attend the opening and/or analysis of the B-sample is fatal to the doping control process and will invalidate the finding that an ADRV has been committed.

C. The Unsatisfied Pre-conditions Argument

441. Athlete 1 cited the then IAAF Rule 45.3 as the basis for the second limb of her argument. The Rule stated: 'The Council may, on behalf of all Members, recognise Testing in the sport of Athletics by a body that is not a Signatory under rules and procedures different from those in the Anti-Doping Rules and Regulations, if it is satisfied that the Testing was properly carried out and that the rules of the body conducting the Testing are otherwise consistent with the Anti-Doping Rules and Regulations.'

442. On these facts, the testing was done under the joint jurisdiction of the NCAA and Athlete 1's university, which were not Code signatories nor under the authority of the Code. In that regard, Rule 45.3 could be relied upon by the IAAF in its charge against Athlete 1, but with two conditions attached:

(1) that the testing carried out by the NCAA and/or the university was done properly; and
(2) that the rules of the conducting entity were otherwise consistent with the IAAF's Anti-Doping Rules and Regulations.[301]

443. Athlete 1 asserted, *inter alia*, that the failure to afford her the above fundamental rights meant that condition one was not met. Relatedly, she also argued that condition two was not satisfied because of the failure of the NCAA's rules to offer her the right to witness the B-sample laboratory analysis, whether personally or via her representative.

D. The Full Hearing Argument

444. Athlete 1 cited Article 8 of the 2009 Code to establish the third limb of her argument. Article 8 provided, in part, as follows:

> Each Anti-Doping Organization with responsibility for results management shall provide a hearing process for any Person who is asserted to have committed an anti-doping rule violation. Such hearing process shall address whether an anti-doping rule violation was committed and, if so, the appropriate Consequences. The hearing process shall respect the following principles:

301. *Ibid.*, at 8.

- a timely hearing;
- a fair and impartial hearing panel …
- the right to be informed in a fair and timely manner of the asserted anti-doping rule violation;
- the right to respond to the asserted anti-doping rule violation and resulting Consequences;
- the right of each party to present evidence, including the right to call and question witnesses (subject to the hearing panel's discretion to accept testimony by telephone or written submission).

445. When read together with Rule 33.1 of the IAAF Rules it meant, according to Athlete 1, that it was mandatory that she be afforded a hearing in which she could challenge the reliability of the evidence brought against her. It also meant that the prosecuting authority bore the burden of proving the reliability of the evidence and the guilt of the athlete to the comfortable satisfaction of the adjudicatory panel.[302]

446. Athlete 1's case, under this head, was that the prosecuting authority failed to produce critical laboratory documentation at the hearing, thus denied her the right to challenge and test that evidence. In other words, if there was documentation to prove an adverse analytical finding, then she should have been able to see it and challenge. She asserted that she was never given that opportunity, all of this against her underlying denial of knowingly ingesting MHA.

E. The Decision of the Disciplinary Committee of the NAAATT

447. On 30 May 2013, the Disciplinary Committee of the NAAATT issued its decision in the matter. There were a few noteworthy ancillary matters highlighted in the ruling, such as the question as to who really had proper results management authority in the case, given Athlete 1's status as an international-level athlete.

448. The salient sections of the decision are found in paragraphs 37 and 38:

> [T]he Committee concludes that by failing to allow the Athlete to be present at the analysis or testing of the B-sample, and by failing to provide the laboratory package when requested by the Athlete, the NCAA as testing authority did not comply with the WADA Code and the IAAF Rules. As a consequence, the result of the B-sample analysis is invalidated and cannot be used to confirm the A-sample result.
>
> No anti-doping rule violation has therefore been committed by the Athlete resulting in no imposition of a sanction and a recommendation for the lifting of the provisional suspension in effect since February 27, 2013. The Committee concludes by repeating, mutatis mutandis, the words of the CAS Panel at

302. *Ibid.*, p. 10.

paragraph 9.25 of Wen Tong: '… *the Panel is not declaring that the Appellant did or did not, voluntarily or not, ingest clenbuterol. The Panel is merely concluding that the Respondent has not been able to prove, to the comfortable satisfaction of the Panel, diligent adherence to the rules set out in the applicable anti-doping regulations.*' [Emphasis original]

449. The Disciplinary Committee accepted the submissions of Athlete 1 and ruled in her favour. The IAAF appealed this decision to the CAS.

F. The IAAF's Appeal

450. The main reliefs sought by the IAAF in its appeal to CAS were:

(1) that Athlete 1 be adjudged to have committed a second ADRV involving the use of MHA and/or the presence of MHA;
(2) that she be given an appropriate period of ineligibility for her second ADRV in accordance with the range specified in the applicable regulations, namely, the 2012–2013 IAAF Competition Rules;[303]
(3) that she be adjudged to have engaged in aggravating circumstances through deceptive conduct at the NAAATT hearing within the meaning of IAAF Rule 40.6 such that her period of ineligibility should be increased;
(4) that her competitive results from the date of the positive test be disqualified and that her prizes, appearance money, awards and titles be forfeited.

451. In instituting the appeal proceedings in which they sought a de novo hearing of all the issues, the IAAF re-suspended Athlete 1 with immediate effect.

G. The Grounds of Appeal and the Response of the NAAATT

452. A further exchange of written submissions first by the IAAF in the form on an Appeal Brief and then by the NAAATT in answer to the Appeal Brief raised doubts about Athlete 1's testimony before the Disciplinary Committee of the NAAATT. In summary, the IAAF's primary assertion was that Athlete 1 was, in fact, present at her B-Sample analysis for at least two hours and that she voluntarily left the process before its completion.

453. The NAAATT Disciplinary Committee believed the assertions raised by the IAAF in its Appeal Brief, which then became the catalyst for the settlement agreement before the CAS hearing took place.

---

303. Chapter 3, Art. 40.7.

H. Comment

454. The case involving Athlete 1 was the first high-profile doping case in Trinidad and Tobago. On one hand, it is unfortunate that the matter was not fully ventilated before a CAS Panel as the ruling would have offered very useful legal instruction and expertise for the country and, by extension, the region as far as doping jurisprudence is concerned. On the other hand, the fact of a pre-hearing settlement probably prevented even further negative publicity for Athlete 1 in a country that is so small that the adverse social impact of a positive drug test can potentially be devastating.

455. One of the interesting legal questions raised in the appeal submissions, and for which CAS guidance would have been instructive, was whether a disciplinary committee was also a prosecuting authority. The NAAATT posed the question in its submissions and sought to answer it in the following way:

> The NAAA holds the view that the role of a disciplinary committee in general and an anti-doping disciplinary panel in particular is standard. It is well established both within and outside of the sporting arena that due process safeguards, including the respect of natural justice principles, must be a central feature of the disciplinary process.
>
> IAAF Rule 38.7 stipulates that '*Every Athlete shall have the right to request a hearing before the relevant tribunal of his National Federation before any sanction is determined in accordance with these Anti-Doping Rules.*' [Athlete 1], through her legal counsel, did request such a hearing which was granted to her.
>
> Rule 38.7 further states which principles should be respected during the hearing process, including a timely hearing, a fair and impartial tribunal, the right to be represented by counsel, the right to respond to an assertion of an anti-doping rule violation and the right to present evidence. The role of the disciplinary panel, then, is to ensure that the above principles are indeed respected. Further, the hearing process itself, by its definition, is intended to be inquisitorial and not adversarial. (*French vs Australian Sports Commission and Cycling Australia*, CAS 2004/A/651)
>
> IAAF Rule 38.12 is instructive outlining that '[a]t the hearing of the Athlete's case, the relevant tribunal shall consider first whether or not an anti-doping rule violation has been committed. The Member or other prosecuting authority shall have the burden of proving the anti-doping rule violation to the comfortable satisfaction of the tribunal.'
>
> The language of Rule 38.12 suggests that the disciplinary tribunal is a separate entity from the prosecuting authority. The IAAF Appeal Brief erroneously seeks to make the disciplinary panel act as a prosecuting authority which is not its function. The function of the NAAA Panel was to weigh the evidence before it and to decide, whether to its comfortable satisfaction, an anti-doping rule violation was committed by the Athlete. On the current facts, the missing prosecuting authority appears to have been the NCAA.

In *G. v FEI* (CAS 91/53, Award of 15 January, 1992), it was established that sports governing bodies do not enjoy investigative rights so that especially in doping cases, the basis of a charge is typically, the analysis done by the relevant laboratory. The NAAA Panel, a tribunal appointed by the NAAA, the national governing body for athletics in Trinidad and Tobago, cannot then be asked to exercise powers of investigation. Simply put, that was not and still is not its function, as has been suggested by the IAAF in its Appeal Brief.[304] [Emphasis original]

456. In other words, the issue raised by the NAAATT concerned the true nature of a disciplinary tribunal in the context of an anti-doping hearing. Due to the fact that a settlement ensued, the IAAF did not get an opportunity to respond to the NAAATT's assertions about the limited scope of the functions of a disciplinary committee.

457. Perhaps this was the only down side to the internal resolution of this case. A CAS ruling would have taken sports law in Trinidad and Tobago one step further, in what must still be considered the early stages of the development of this area of academic study in the country.

§2. CAS 2014/A/3731

458. The second major doping case emanating from Trinidad and Tobago was also resolved in advance of a final hearing before the CAS. A confidential Consent Award was issued after the disputing parties and their legal representatives reached an agreement.

459. The Athlete in this case (hereinafter referred to as 'Athlete 2') accepted the commission of the ADRV, although she articulated that there was no intent to cheat on her part. It is now well known that since the adoption and implementation of the 2015 Code, the question of intention to cheat can have a direct bearing on the length of the period of ineligibility imposed on the offending party.

I. The Local Hearing: Decision of the NAAATT Disciplinary Committee

460. The key issue for determination before the Disciplinary Committee of the NAAATT[305] was whether the assistance provided by Athlete 2 could be considered 'Substantial Assistance' within the meaning of Rule 40.5(c) of the IAAF's Anti-Doping Rules. That Rule stated, in part, as follows:

---

304. NAAATT Answer to the IAAF Appeal brief, pages 9–10, paras 23–27.
305. This Panel was chaired by the author of this book.

> The relevant tribunal of a Member may, prior to a final appellate decision under Rule 42 of the expiration of the time to appeal (where applicable in the case of an International-Level Athlete having referred the matter to the Doping Review Board for its determination under Rule 38.16) suspend a part of the period of Ineligibility imposed in an individual case where the Athlete or other Person has provided Substantial Assistance to the IAAF, his National Federation, an Anti-Doping Organisation, criminal authority or professional disciplinary body resulting in the IAAF, National Federation or Anti-Doping Organisation discovering or establishing an anti-doping rule violation by another Person or resulting in a criminal or disciplinary body discovering or establishing a criminal offence or the breach of professional rules by another Person.[306]

461. The spirit and intent of this rule is to encourage a certain degree of whistle-blowing, with the consequence that the whistle-blower may receive a reduction in the otherwise applicable period of ineligibility.

462. In the current case, the disciplinary tribunal had to determine three main issues:

(1) In view of the fact that there was no dispute as to the commission of an ADRV, whether exceptional or special circumstances existed, sufficient to justify the elimination or reduction of any applicable period of ineligibility.
(2) If such exceptional or special circumstances existed, what would be the applicable period of ineligibility?
(3) What would be the commencement date of that period of ineligibility?

463. In its Interim Award, the local tribunal referred to the decision in *Knauss v. FIS*,[307] and made the following pronouncements:

> In the *Knauss* award, the CAS Panel noted at Paragraph 23 that the '*purpose of Article 10.5.3 FIS-Rules is primarily to treat an athlete preferentially who contributes to the discovery and elimination of certain prohibited activities.*' It further noted at Paragraph 25 that the '*intention of Article 10.5.3 FIS-Rules is to grant preferential treatment to athletes who, by furnishing information, contribute towards the fight against doping in their immediate environment. The motive for this preferential treatment is the recognition that the instruments for*

306. 'Substantial Assistance' as defined in the IAAF Competition Rules provides that 'For the purposes of Rule 40.5(c), a Person providing Substantial Assistance must (i) fully disclose in a signed written statement all information he possesses in relation to ADRVs and (ii) fully co-operate with the investigation and adjudication of any case related to that information, including, for example, presenting testimony at a hearing if requested to do so by the prosecuting authority or hearing panel. Further, the information provided must be credible and must comprise an important part of any case which is initiated or, if no case is initiated, must have provided a sufficient basis on which a case could have been brought.'
307. CAS 2005/A/847.

> *combating and eliminating the acts of trafficking, possession or the administration of prohibited substances are extremely limited. This is due primarily to the inherently clandestine nature of these activities and, secondly, the personal relationships which the athlete usually has developed to the people and athletes in his immediate proximity. The athlete will generally not want to expose these persons to the risk of a sanction. Article 10.5.3 FIS-Rules is intended to create an incentive for the athlete to provide the information which is urgently required for the fight against doping.*'[308] [Emphasis original]

464. The NAAATT's tribunal, therefore, reviewed the sparse case law available on the issue of Substantial Assistance, while also considering previous cases addressing special or exceptional circumstances. Athlete 2 asserted that she did provide substantial assistance enough to warrant the applicable reduction in her ban from competition and the Disciplinary Committee agreed with her. The IAAF appealed that decision to CAS.

II. The IAAF's Appeal

465. The IAAF's appeal to CAS was limited to two issues:

(1) the decision of the NAAATT Disciplinary Committee to begin the period of ineligibility to the date of sample collection, which was in April 2013; and
(2) the decision of the Disciplinary Committee to suspend 12 months of the two-year period of ineligibility imposed on Athlete 2, pursuant to the Substantial Assistance provisions of the IAAF Competition Rules.

466. With respect to the first issue, the IAAF's viewpoint was that there was no basis for the backdating of the commencement date. Regarding the second issue, the IAAF held the view that a more appropriate sanction would have been the suspension of only three months of the twenty-four month period of ineligibility.

467. As was the case with Athlete 1, the parties reached a settlement agreement which eventually led to the issuing of a confidential Consent Award by the CAS, so that there was no final legal determination of the issues raised prior to the scheduled CAS hearing.

III. Comment

468. This was another case in which guidance from the CAS would have been welcome, especially for the benefit of the Caribbean region, where comparatively speaking, there are not many cases heard and determined before the CAS.

308. Interim Award of the NAAATT Disciplinary Panel, p. 11.

469. Especially with regard to the Substantial Assistance provisions of the Code, there is a dearth of sporting jurisprudence to offer guidance on their interpretation and application. For that reason, again, perhaps the only disadvantage of the settlement was the missed opportunity for legal clarity from the CAS on Substantial Assistance cases.

470. It is significant to note the proposals that have been made during the course of the 2021 Code Review process concerning the Substantial Assistance provision. The 2015 Code stipulates that someone who has provided Substantial Assistance may benefit from a suspension of part of the period of ineligibility if that assistance has one of two effects:

(1) the assistance must result in the Anti-Doping Organisation that received the information being able to discover or bring forward an ADRV committed by another person or;
(2) the assistance must result in a criminal or disciplinary body discovering or bringing forward a criminal offence or the breach of professional rules committed by another person. In this second scenario, the information provided by the individual providing the assistance must also be made available to the Anti-Doping Organisation with results management authority.[309]

471. The Second Draft of the 2021 Code adds another two effects which could trigger the Substantial Assistance benefits:

(1) the assistance must result in WADA initiating a proceeding against a Signatory, WADA-accredited laboratory or Athlete Passport Management Unit (APMU)[310] for non-compliance with the Code, International Standard or Technical Document;
(2) the assistance must, with WADA's approval, result in a criminal or disciplinary body bringing forward a criminal offence or the breach of professional or sport rules arising out of a sport integrity violation other than doping.[311]

472. The proposed expansion of this article increases its opportunities to be invoked since there are now four circumstances rather than two in which someone offering Substantial Assistance can benefit. The Comment[312] to the new Article 10.7.1 is instructive stating that the 'cooperation of Athletes, Athlete Support Personnel and other Persons who acknowledge their mistake and are willing to bring other anti-doping rule violations to light is important to clean sport'.

309. Article 10.6.1.1, 2015 Code.
310. The function of the APMU is defined in Annex L of the International Standard for Testing and Investigations.
311. Article 10.7.1.1, 2021 Code, Second Draft dated 10 Dec. 2018.
312. This comment is an abbreviated version of that found in the 2015 Code under Art. 10.6.1.

§3. Conclusion

473. The foregoing recommendation offers a timely reminder of the multifaceted approach that is needed in the ongoing battle for clean sport. Viret[313] noted accurately that this battle brings together the fields of law and science at a fascinating intersection. Citing Mc Laren, her succinct evaluation was noteworthy:

> Anti-doping science constantly needs to progress in order to keep pace with new drugs and newly emerging doping practices. The proficiency of anti-doping laboratories in their field and their speed in developing new analytical methods or refining their analytical tools is of paramount importance for the effectiveness of the fight against doping. However, the science used must be sufficiently robust to support the prosecution of an anti-doping rule violation and withstand the scrutiny of a court or other judicial body in the judicial process.[314]

474. These are useful perspectives which lucidly capture the primacy of scientific evidence and juxtaposes it against the rigour of legal scrutiny. The way forward in seeking to reduce and/or eliminate drug use in sport will continue to bring these two fields together with the hope that the gap will continue to close between offender and regulator.

313. Marjolaine Viret, *Evidence in Anti-Doping at the Intersection of Science and Law* (Springer 2016).
314. *Ibid.*, p. 409.

Part IV. Sport and Commerce

Chapter 1. General Issues

475. It is an ineluctable fact that the global sports industry of the modern era is a hugely lucrative one, valued in the billions of dollars, pounds or euros. The rapid commercialisation of the sports sector over the past three or so decades has quickly moved the practice of sport from amateur to professional, from hobby to vocation.

476. Against this backdrop, four major revenue streams have emerged in sport, namely, sponsorship, broadcasting rights, merchandising and ticketing. In the midst of this evolution has also been the emergence of the pivotal role of intellectual property rights in sport with copyright and trademark law, in particular, standing out as the catalyst upon which valuable sports rights are created and monetised.

477. In this section of the monograph, the foregoing commercial elements of sport will be examined, with special attention being placed on how these rights have been protected when Trinidad and Tobago has organised and/or hosted major sporting events. The following events will be kept in view:

- The ICC Cricket World Cup, West Indies, 2007
- The FIFA Under-17 Men's World Cup, 2001
- The FIFA Under-17 Women's World Cup, 2010
- The Caribbean Premier League, 2017–2020
- The Caribbean Games 2009[315] and
- The 2021 Commonwealth Youth Games (CYG).

478. A natural overflow of this discussion of event hosting is the legal protection available for the event organiser and the cast of sports rights holders affiliated with the event. In this light, Part V of this monograph will also address the role of intellectual property law in assisting sports rights holders in the attempts to combat ambush marketing, a significant threat to the value of their rights.

479. At the beginning of October 2018, the Minister of Finance indicated in his budget presentation for the Fiscal Year 2018/2019 that the sport sector would be

315. These Games were aborted before the commencement date due to the impending threat of the 'swine flu' disease in Trinidad and Tobago in 2009.

granted approximately TTD 280 million (USD 40 million).[316] Notably, this allocation represented an increase of TTD 20 million (approximately USD 3 million) from the previous fiscal year.[317] For a country of just over 1.3 million people, it is hard to measure whether this amount is too much, too little or just right. Whatever the diagnosis, the general sentiment in Trinidad and Tobago is that the country has not even scratched the surface of its economic potential within the sports industry, especially in the area of sports tourism. These and related issues will be addressed in the following chapters.

316. Mark Pouchet, *$280 m for Sport*, Trinidad Express, https://www.trinidadexpress.com/sports/local/m-for-sport/article_208540a0-c5dd-11e8-a36c-8bd17de1d024.html, 1 Oct. 2018.
317. *Ibid.*

Chapter 2. The Organisation of Events

§1. Introduction

480. There is unquestionable appeal associated with some of the world's major sporting spectacles, whether the event in question is a single-game event like the Super Bowl, a single-sport event like the Rugby World Cup or a multisport event like the Asian Games. One corollary of this appeal is that event organisers have increasingly shown their grasp of the intrinsic value of being a host. Notwithstanding recent reticence shown by some nations, especially for financial reasons, Olympic bidding, for instance, still remains an intriguing process and a prize to be pursued. A similar reality also exists for the FIFA World Cup.

481. Yet, even a tier or two below the prestige of the Olympics and the World Cup, interest remains high for other events like the Commonwealth Games, CYG, the Youth Olympic Games, the Africa Cup of Nations and the IAAF World Championships.

482. In recent months, Trinidad and Tobago has expressed an interest in hosting the CYG in 2021. Inspired perhaps by the success of Caribbean neighbours, the Bahamas, in hosting the 2017 edition of the CYG, Trinidad and Tobago has thrown its proverbial 'hat in the ring',[318] noting that the estimated hosting cost would be in the vicinity of TTD 4 million (approximately USD 600,000).[319]

483. Should this be pursued and should there be ensuing success, it would not be the first time that the country has hosted a major sporting event. Yet, host nations today are quite aware that staging an event brings with it the need for robust measures to ensure proper legal regulation and logistical planning together with an effective post-event legacy strategy. Intellectual property (IP) law is an essential cog in the event delivery wheel.

§2. Sport and Intellectual Property

484. Undoubtedly, the role that IP law now plays in the sports sector is a pivotal one. IP rights have become a basis for significant revenue-generating potential for athletes, especially at the end of their playing careers. Global superstars like former England football captain David Beckham and basketball's American icon Michael Jordan, continue to earn significant sums of money many years after they hung up their shoes. Such is the power of IP rights in sport.

---

318. *Trinidad and Tobago Consider Bid for 2021 Commonwealth Youth Games*, https://www.ttoc.org/index.php/international-games/commonwealth-games/7028-trinidad-and-tobago-consider-bid-for-2021-commonwealth-youth-games, 24 June 2018.

319. Mark Pouchet, *TTOC Needs $4 Million to Host Youth Games*, Trinidad Express, https://www.trinidadexpress.com/sports/local/ttoc-needs-us-m-to-host-youth-games/article_ff878e02-d730-11e8-9c21-873a54408dcb.html, 23 Oct. 2018.

I. Copyright and Trademarks: Statutory Definitions

485. There are many useful definitions of the term 'copyright' across the academic spectrum. Writing from a US perspective, Walter Champion has defined copyright law as the law that 'protects original works of authorship embodied in a tangible medium of expression',[320] adding that certain subject matter is protected by copyright law such as music, drama, computer programmes, sound recordings and the visual arts.[321]

486. From a UK perspective, Lewis and Taylor have noted that pursuant to section 1 of the 1988 Copyright Design and Patents Act, 'copyright subsists in original literary, dramatic, musical and artistic works; sound recordings, films, broadcasts and cable programmes; and the typographical arrangements of published editions'.[322] The 1988 Act in section 2(1) confers exclusive rights upon the copyright holder in relation to the stated acts which include copying, renting, broadcasting and making the particular work available to the public.

487. One of the key features of copyright is that it subsists automatically, with no registration requirement needed for its enforceability. In Trinidad and Tobago, the applicable legislation is the 1997 Copyright Act, Chapter 82:80. The 1997 Act defines copyright in some detail according to section 5(1):

> Copyright is a property right which subsists in literary and artistic works that are original intellectual creations in the literary and artistic domain, including in particular— (a) books, pamphlets, articles, computer programs and other writings; (b) speeches, lectures, addresses, sermons and other works of the same nature; (c) dramatic works, dramatico-musical works, pantomimes, choreographic works and other works created for stage productions; (d) stage productions of works mentioned in paragraph (c); (e) musical works, with or without accompanying words; (f) audio-visual works; (g) works of architecture; (h) works of drawing, painting, sculpture, engraving, lithography, tapestry and other works of fine art; (i) photographic works; (j) works of applied art; (k) illustrations, maps, plans, sketches and three dimensional works relative to geography, topography, architecture or science.'

488. Section 5(2) adds that: 'Works shall be protected by the sole fact of their creation and irrespective of their mode or form of expression, as well as of their content, quality and purpose.' This is the above-mentioned automatic creation of the right without the need for formalities.

---

320. Walter T. Champion, Jr, at page 534, *Sports Law in a Nutshell* 534 (West Academic Publishing 5th ed. 2017).
321. *Ibid.*
322. Lewis and Taylor, *supra*, n. 220, at 1707, para. I 1.61.

489. Section 8(1) expands on the nature of copyright and goes on to establish the exclusivity granted to the copyright owner. In Trinidad and Tobago, that exclusivity whether to authorise or to prohibit a particular type of activity relates to the following:

- reproduction of the work;
- translation of the work;
- adaptation, arrangement or other transformation of the work;
- the first public distribution of the original and each copy of the work by sale, rental or otherwise;
- rental or public lending of the original or a copy of an audio-visual work, a work embodied in a sound recording, a computer programme, a database or a musical work in the form of notation, irrespective of the ownership of the original or copy concerned;
- importation of copies of the work, even where the imported copies were made with the authorisation of the owner of copyright;
- public display of the original or a copy of the work;
- public performance of the work;
- broadcasting of the work; or
- communication to the public of the work.

490. The sum total of the foregoing sections is that copyright owners in Trinidad and Tobago, as in other territories, can seek to protect the attendant exclusivity afforded to them, by invoking the respective provisions of the Act. As long as the copyright owner can illustrate that he has used his own labour, skill, judgment and effort in creating the protected work, he is likely to enjoy strong legal protection. As noted by the court in *Ladbroke (Football) Ltd. v. William Hill (Football) Ltd,*[323] it has 'often been recognised that if sufficient skill and judgment have been exercised in devising the arrangements of the whole work, that can be an important or even decisive element in deciding whether the work as a whole is protected by copyright'.[324]

491. These principles were endorsed in *Full Blown Entertainment Company Limited v. Devon Matthews and others (2017),*[325] where the High Court of Trinidad and Tobago made the following pronouncements in relation to copyright:

> In matters, such as the one before this Court, the Claimant has an obligation to satisfy the Court on a balance of probabilities that his work was actually copied and secondly that the copying of same was executed without the requisite authorisation and that the use of protected material was in the circumstances improper and/or unlawful.
>
> Direct or circumstantial evidence must be advanced to establish that the alleged infringer actually had access to the protected work and the evidence

323. [1964] 1 W.L.R. 273.
324. *Ibid.*, p. 277.
325. Claim No. CV 2015-01073.

> must also establish that the alleged infringing work is substantially similar to the protected work, which must itself be work that was original, unique and capable of attracting the requisite intellectual property protection.[326]

492. Here, the court, *inter alia*, spoke about the need for the work to be original and unique if legal protection were to be available to the Claimant. In particular, as the court examined whether words used in a song were substantially similar to the original work, it concluded that the words under review were not a unique literary expression that could attract copyright protection. This was because the court did not find any original skill, labour or originality of thought associated with the words in question.[327]

493. Koo's recent analysis of *Full Blown Entertainment* is instructive, as he cited some of the key legal issues arising from the judgment:

> As a matter of the facts and law before the court, this was the right decision. However, two interesting points arise. It was curious to see the judge depart from the traditional phrase 'labour, skill and judgement' that is common to the UK copyright case law. It is uncertain whether this was a deliberate move to set an 'originality' threshold different to that of the UK approach or simply an interchangeable use of language. Furthermore, the concluding sentence of paragraph 71 seemingly left it open that phrases can be subject to copyright protection in Trinidad. Seepersad J. stated: 'the phrase is not a unique literary expression which can attract copyright protection'. From this, it appears that a 'unique literary expression' can be subject to copyright protection. The use of the word 'unique', prima facie suggests some essence of novelty. However, this has never been a requirement for copyright law. Therefore, it is uncertain what threshold this sets for copyright protection. Moreover, the uncertainty extends to the question whether there is conflict between the phrase 'unique literary expression' and the 'originality' requirement previously expressed: 'original skill, labour or originality of thought'. It is unknown whether 'unique literary expression' comes within the scope of 'originality of thought' or whether a separate threshold is established for the protection of phrases. Consequently, there is a need to clarify the 'originality' requirement under Trinidad copyright law.[328]

494. It is as a result of the foregoing observations that Koo considered the court to have missed an opportunity both to add clarity and to advance the law of copyright in Trinidad and Tobago.

---

326. *Ibid.*, at paras 24 and 25.
327. *Ibid.*, at para. 71.
328. Justin Koo, *Full Blown Entertainment: A Missed Opportunity for Advancing the Copyright Law of Developing Commonwealth Countries with Hybrid Copyright Systems*, 13 *J. Intellectual Property Law & Practice* (2018).

A. Communication to the Public and Blocking Injunctions

495. Copyright law in modern times has seen a dramatic increase in the number of cases where the right to communicate to the public has been under review. Notably, the jurisprudential developments have stemmed primarily from football-related cases, starting with *QC Leisure*[329] and exploding with myriad other cases involving the Football Association Premier League (FAPL). Article 3 of the Copyright and Information Society Directive (Directive 2001/29/EC) was considered before the England and Wales High Court in *QC Leisure*. Article 3(1) stated that Member States 'shall provide authors with the exclusive right to authorize or prohibit any communication to the public of their works, by wire or wireless means, including the making available to the public of their works in such a way that members of the public may access them from a place and at a time individually chosen by them'. The wording of this provision closely mirrored that of Article 8 of the WIPO[330] Copyright Treaty.

496. On the facts of *QC Leisure*, the court had to interpret whether the owner of a pub in showing Premier League football matches to patrons, communicated to the public works protected by copyright. Kitchin J.'s provisional view was that no such communication had taken place. This question, evidently, was one of a series of questions referred to the CJEU. The CJEU responded by stating that 'the answer to the question referred is that "communication to the public" within the meaning of Article 3(1) of the Copyright Directive must be interpreted as covering transmission of the broadcast works, via television screen and speakers, to the customers present in a public house'.[331]

497. The courts of Trinidad and Tobago are yet to rule on this matter in the context of sports so that these developments have great potential to shape the future of sports law in the country. Similar precedent-setting opportunities can also emerge from the recent line of 'live' injunction (blocking injunction) cases involving British Telecommunications.

498. As in the other FAPL cases, the FAPL owned the copyright in films comprising television footage of matches in the English Premier League as well as the copyright in artistic works that appeared within that footage.[332] The FAPL approached the court seeking an injunction that would prohibit service providers from infringing their copyright through unlawful streaming of the football matches. In granting the order the court not only considered it to be proportionate but also found that the interference in the defendant's business was 'justified by a legitimate aim, namely preventing infringement of FAPL's copyrights on a large scale'.[333]

329. *Football Association Premier League and others v. QC Leisure and others* [2008] EWHC 1411 (Ch).
330. WIPO.
331. Joined Cases C-403/08, C-429/08 at para. 207, p. 31.
332. *FAPL Ltd. v. British Telecommunications Plc* [2017 EWHC 480 (Ch).
333. *Ibid*, para. 69, p. 13.

Even more recently in July 2018, Arnold J. in *FAPL v. British Telecommunications and others*[334] extended the blocking injunction to cover the 2018/2019 Premier League season. In September 2018, the blocking order approach was carried over to the sport of boxing in *Matchroom Boxing Ltd and another v. British Telecommunications.*[335]

499. These 'live' injunction cases have presented an alternative remedy for copyright holders, especially in the realm of sports broadcasting. IP regulators in Trinidad and Tobago will welcome this new jurisprudential trend.

II. Sport and Trademark Law

500. With respect to trademarks, the applicable law in Trinidad and Tobago is the Trade Marks Act Chapter 82:81. In that Act, 'trademark' has been defined as 'a mark used or proposed to be used in relation to goods for the purpose of indicating, or so as to indicate, a connection in the course of trade between the goods and some person having the right either as proprietor or as registered user to use the mark, whether with or without any indication of the identity of that person'.[336] In other words, the trademark connects the owner to the goods in question, with this connection occurring in the course of trade. It is a commercially based nexus.

501. According to section 9 of the Trade Marks Act, there is a registration requirement in order for legal protection to ensue for the rights owner. This distinguishes this form of IP from copyright for which there is no such registration requirement.

502. Distinctiveness is a key feature for successful trademark registration. Section 10 of the Trade Marks Act defines 'distinctiveness' to mean something that has been 'adapted, in relation to the goods in respect of which a trademark is registered or proposed to be registered, to distinguish goods with which the proprietor of the trademark is or may be connected in the course of trade from goods in the case of which no such connection subsists, either generally or, where the trademark is registered or proposed to be registered subject to limitations, in relation to use within the extent of the registration'.

503. This requirement of distinctiveness is pivotal in trademark registration and its absence can be fatal to the application process. Johnson has given prudent advice in this regard suggesting that:

334. [2018] EWHC 1828 (Ch).
335. [2018] EWHC 2443 (Ch).
336. Section 2.

in relation to a major sporting event an application should be considered for at least the following word marks:

> EVENT + YEAR [e.g. WORLD CUP 2006]
> EVENT + LOCATION [e.g. WORLD CUP GERMANY]
> EVENT +NO [e.g. 12th FINA WORLD CHAMPIONSHIP]
> EVENT [e.g. RUGBY WORLD CUP or WIMBLEDON]
> LOCATION + YEAR [e.g. LONDON 2012].[337]

504. Johnson has added that it is not uncommon to see candidate cities beginning the application process to register certain trademarks as a way of enhancing their bid.[338] In the build up to the 2006 football World Cup in Germany, the Office for Harmonisation in the Internal Market (OHIM) upheld the registration of GERMANY 2006, WORLD CUP GERMANY, WORLD CUP 2006 and WM 2006.[339] He noted that in relation to this application the OHIM 'took the view that although the marks consisting of a year *simpliciter*, or the use of a particular geographical location (Germany) may not be distinctive or may be descriptive of the goods and services, this did not apply to the four marks in suit. In particular, it held that GERMANY 2006 does not describe a football championship since this does not appear in the mark; it is only suggestive of something happening in Germany or of a world championship that will take place in Germany'. He added that, in part, 'these decisions relied on the fact that the two words did not form a grammatically correct expression and so they could not be descriptive of that event. The fact that the marks were suggestive of the tournament does not mean that they are devoid of distinctive character'.[340]

505. Since that time, event organisers appear to have the settled practice of adding the event logo to word marks, an approach which further cements the distinctiveness requirement. It is no surprise to see the trademark combinations of PARIS 2024 and LA 2028 with their respective logos as they prepare to host their corresponding editions of the Summer Olympics. Notably, even without the logo FIFA has registered the phrase 2022 FIFA World Cup Qatar. In such instances one can typically expect to find the symbol '®' placed next to the registered mark to confirm its registration or the symbol 'TM' to confirm its use as a trademark.

506. It is in this regard that trademark law has become a true ally of event organisers in the face of the real threat of ambush marketing. Trinidad and Tobago as a past host nation has gained significant IP experience in recent years as it hosted

337. Phillip Johnson, *Ambush Marketing: A Practical Guide to Protecting the Brand of a Sporting Event* 16 (EIPR Practice Series, Book 1, Thomson, Sweet & Maxwell 2007).
338. *Ibid.*
339. *Ibid.*, p. 22.
340. *Ibid.*

sports events of varying degrees of prominence and magnitude, the standout occasion being the 2007 ICC's CWC ('CWC 2007'). This and other events will be assessed in the following paragraphs.

III. The ICC Cricket World Cup 2007

507. Trinidad and Tobago was one of nine host countries to welcome the cricketing world to Caribbean shores in early 2007. It may very well have been the first time that a global sporting event of such a scale was hosted across so many countries. This is, of course, no longer a novel initiative with joint bids becoming a regular occurrence in event hosting, as evidenced most recently by the successful joint bid of Mexico, Canada and the US for the hosting of the 2026 Senior Men's FIFA World Cup.

508. The legislative framework for CWC 2007 displayed predictable consistency across the region as the primary statute, the ICC CWC West Indies 2007 Act, 2006 (the 'CWC Act') was drafted under the guidance of the CARICOM Legal Affairs Committee. This ensured a welcome degree of harmonisation across host nations.

509. In Trinidad and Tobago, there were several provisions of the legislation that offered sound protection of the commercial rights of the ICC and its primary partners. Even the definition section of the legislation demonstrated the depth to which the legislative drafters were willing to go in order to offer the best statutory protection possible.

510. From a trademark law perspective and by way of illustration, 'CWC mark' was defined as:

> the CWC 2007 logo, CWC 2007 title, CWC 2007 mascot, and the image or likeness of the CWC 2007 trophy, the ICC mark, any mark belonging to WICB and any other marks, whether in the form of words, logos, devices, indicia, or anything else, developed for or used by or with the consent of IDI[341] in connection with the CWC 2007, and includes all registrations or applications to register the same in Trinidad and Tobago but excludes any such marks to the extent that they are owned by an official sponsor, official supplier, official broadcaster or other media or commercial representative appointed by GCC or CWC 2007 Inc. and approved by IDI;

511. This broad definition of a 'CWC mark' sought to capture the intellectual property belonging to the ICC, the WICB (now called 'Cricket West Indies'), the ICC Developmental (International) Limited (IDI) and the Global Cricket Corporation, a company incorporated under the laws of Singapore.

341. ICC Development (International) Limited.

512. The width of the definition of a 'CWC mark' takes us back to the purpose of a trademark pursuant to the interpretation section of the Trade Marks Act which was originally drafted in 1955, with subsequent amendments. Such a mark is used or proposed to be used so as to indicate a connection between the relevant goods and their proprietor in the course of trade. It is instructive to note the change to the definition of trademark in the 2015 Trade Marks Act of Trinidad and Tobago which was drafted to repeal the 1955 Act but which is yet to be proclaimed. The 2015 Act defines it as 'any sign capable of being represented graphically and which is capable of distinguishing goods or services dealt with or provided in the course of trade by a person, from goods or services so dealt with or provided by any other person',[342] therefore bringing it in line with the EU approach to trademarks.

513. This latter definition changes the point of focus from connection to distinction. There is a further definition in 2015 of a 'well-known trademark' which means:

> (a) any registered trade mark that is well known in Trinidad and Tobago; or (b) any unregistered trade mark that is well known in Trinidad and Tobago and that belongs to a person who is— (i) a national of a Convention country; or (ii) domiciled in, or has a real and effective industrial or commercial establishment in, a Convention country, whether or not that person carries on business, or has any goodwill, in Trinidad and Tobago.

514. It is submitted that the modern definition accords with the changed commercial and business environment generally, including that of the sports sector. Additionally, prima facie, owners of both registered and unregistered sports-related trademarks have broader protection in Trinidad and Tobago by virtue of the expanded definition.

A. *Sponsorship and Ambush Marketing*

515. For the most part, it is fair to say that outside of persons within the business sector and perhaps some academics, many persons in Trinidad and Tobago and, indeed, the wider Caribbean, may have heard about ambush marketing for the first time in the years leading up to CWC 2007. Yet, by the time the event rolled around, the educational emphasis of the ICC, WICB and Local Organising Committee would have paid dividends in making persons more aware of this commercial threat.

516. The Trinidad and Tobago legislation offered a comprehensive definition of the term in section 25(1) and (2) of the CWC Act:

> Except with the written authorization of CWC 2007 Inc., IDI or GCC a person shall not wilfully broadcast, display, make, publish or televise any advertisement, communication, statement, mark or image or cause or authorize any

342. Section 3(1).

advertisement, communication, statement, mark or image to be broadcast, displayed, made, published, televised or carried on, cause or authorize any other activity which—

(a) relates to or is connected with CWC 2007;
(b) implies or suggests a contractual or other connection or association of that person with CWC 2007 or a person officially associated or involved in CWC 2007; and
(c) is intended to—
 (i) associate that person with CWC 2007 or exploit the publicity or goodwill of CWC 2007, in order for that person to gain a benefit of any kind;
 (ii) diminish the status of an official sponsor, official supplier, official broadcaster or other licensee with regard to CWC 2007; or
 (iii) imply that the person is an official sponsor, official supplier, official broadcaster or other licensee with regard to CWC 2007.
 (2) No person shall, in relation to CWC 2007, use or cause to be used, a mark, image, statement or brand in a manner calculated to achieve publicity for that mark, image, statement or brand with which that mark, image, statement or brand is associated and thereby deriving any special promotional benefit from CWC 2007 without the prior authority of CWC 2007 Inc. or IDI.

517. A close examination of the above provisions reveals how careful the legislative drafters were in identifying what would be commercially unlawful during the event. This is the heart of the ambush marketing threat. It is the attempt of persons or entities with no official connection to the event, and crucially, with no financial investment having been made, to associate with the prestige of the event.

518. Particular expressions in the foregoing provisions reinforce that point such as:

(1) 'implies or suggests a contractual or other connection or association';
(2) 'exploit the publicity or goodwill of';
(3) 'diminish the status of an official sponsor'; and
(4) 'calculated to achieve publicity'.

519. The wording commendably reflects a sound understanding of how an official commercial partner's status could have been compromised by activity that was calculated to piggy-back on the goodwill of the 2007 tournament. Notwithstanding the fact that this was merely sunset legislation, with its legal effect ending on 30 June 2007, this Act remains a very useful resource for future sports event legislative drafting for the country.

520. There were no officially reported cases of attempts to ambush the CWC 2007 in Trinidad and Tobago. A different approach to the protection of commercial rights was taken, however, for the Under-17 FIFA World Cups.

IV. The FIFA Under-17 World Cups: A Brief Note

521. CWC 2007 was sandwiched between two other sporting events of note in Trinidad and Tobago. In 2001, the country hosted the FIFA Under-17 Men's World Cup, while in 2010, the FIFA Under-17 Women's World Cup was brought to this island's shores. Neither event was hosted against a backdrop of ambush marketing legislation.

522. It appeared to be the case that for both events, the respective Local Organizing Committees were able to rely on educational and awareness campaigns, together with on-site patrols from local law enforcement authorities to police event venues. Evidently, although both events were rather popular, with the 2001 event boasting the likes of Spain's Fernando Torres, France's Florent Sinama Pongolle and Argentina's Carlos Tevez, for instance, their magnitude did not warrant Parliamentary intervention, but instead non-legislative safeguards.

523. Discussions among legal authorities for the latter event led to the conclusion that reliance could be placed on the 1997 Copyright Act, the 1955 Trade Marks Act and the 1997 Protection against Unfair Competition Act to address any potential threats of unlawful use of FIFA's intellectual property in Trinidad and Tobago.

V. The Caribbean Games 2009

524. Just before the hosting of the 2010 FIFA Under-17 Women's World Cup, Trinidad and Tobago was scheduled to stage a five-sport event to be called the Caribbean Games 2009 (CG 2009). This inaugural edition of the event, not to be confused with the already existing Central American and Caribbean (CAC) Games, was set to take place from 12–19 July 2009.

525. CG 2009 was the brainchild of the Caribbean Association of National Olympic Committees and had the noble intention of bringing together some of the leading athletes from the Caribbean into one venue to compete in track and field, beach and indoor volleyball, netball, tennis and boxing.

526. Planning for the event was well advanced including the execution of various commercial agreements. Sadly, the advent of the H1N1 disease (also known as 'Swine Flu') led to the abrupt cancellation of the Games.[343] From a legal perspective, there was very little complication in triggering the force majeure clauses that formed part of the various contracts.

343. *Romany Explains, Says Sorry for Aborted Games*, 23 June 2009, Trinidad Newsday, https://archives.newsday.co.tt/2009/06/23/romany-explains-says-sorry-for-aborted-games/.

VI. The Caribbean Premier League 2017–2020

527. The Hero CPL has become one of the more popular T20 cricket tournaments in the world, boasting the likes of many international stars. The final match of the 2017 and 2018 editions were both hosted in Trinidad and Tobago at the Brian Lara Cricket Academy, a recently opened venue named after one of Trinidad and Tobago's sporting legends, left-hand batsman Brian Lara.

528. The event organiser is the CPL Ltd while the title sponsor for the CPL is Hero MotoCorp Ltd.[344] By virtue of a hosting agreement signed between the Government of Trinidad and Tobago and the CPL Ltd, Trinidad and Tobago was awarded the right to host the final match for the period 2018–2020.

529. This relationship has afforded the country the opportunity to refine its event hosting expertise but to also expose more stakeholders to the commercial and legal realities associated with modern-day sport.

A. *The Contractual Framework of the CPL*

530. The contractual context in which the annual CPL is held is instructive and offers a useful template for other event hosts. Some of the key definitions in the Hosting/Venue Agreements include the following:

(1) The definition of 'commercial rights' which means 'all commercial rights of any kind whatsoever relating to any Match and/or the League, in each case including without limitation sponsorship, supply of goods and services, merchandising, ticketing, catering, hospitality (except as otherwise set out in this Agreement), broadcasting, licensing and advertising/signage rights'.[345]
(2) The definition of 'League Marks' which means 'all trademarks, trade names, logos, symbols, emblems, insignia or slogans or other matters in the nature of intellectual property rights of any kind including copyright used by CPL from time to time in connection with the League including without limitation where the name of the title sponsor is involved'.[346] The term 'Team Marks' has a similar definition which seeks to capture the intellectual property rights associated with each participating team or franchise.
(3) The definition of 'Stadium' which means:

> [T]he whole of the premises of The Brian Lara Stadium and Cricket Academy, Trinidad and Tobago (as detailed in Schedule 6) including without limitation

344. 'Hero Motocorp extends title sponsorship of Hero Caribbean Premier League until 2018', https://www.cplt20.com/sponsors/hero-motocorp-extends-title-sponsorship-hero-caribbean-premier-league-until-2018.
345. Clause 1.3, Stadium Agreement (Trinidad), CPL Finals 2017.
346. *Ibid*, Clause 1.11.

> the Grounds, all accreditation facilities, the areas surrounding the Stadium which falls under the jurisdiction of the stadium, training and warm-up grounds and areas, the stands, passageways, walkways, staircases, lifts, bars, toilets, hospitality facilities, private members' areas, suites, wherever applicable fences, commentary boxes, gantries, walls, windows, seats, boundaries, floodlights, media facilities, electronic scoreboards and replay screens, roofs, shops, box offices, car parks and other areas within the Stadium, airspace above any of the foregoing, static or moving objects inside and outside the Stadium in each case in and around and/or which form part of the Stadium or which are otherwise owned and/or controlled by or otherwise licensed to the Stadium Owner in connection with the Stadium.

531. Such a broad definition of the hosting stadium is noteworthy as the CPL organisers would have seen the commercial potential attached to all aspects of the host venue, including the boundaries of the cricket field and the air space above the stadium. This becomes important when CPL considers its marketing, branding and sponsorship plans as articulated typically in the following language in its Hosting Agreement: 'All commercial exploitation of each Match will be under the control of and belong to CPL and/or CPL Trinidad absolutely. Any normal and/or existing commercial arrangements that the Stadium Owner has for the staging of its own matches or other events at the Stadium will not apply and the Stadium Owner shall make the Stadium available free from any and all commercial obligations or advertising and free from any other restrictions or obligations of any kind whatsoever.'[347]

532. The foregoing provision mirrors the 'clean venue' policy of the IOC during the hosting of the Olympic Games, a philosophy which has its roots in guarding the exclusive rights of an event organiser's official partners. This appears to have become an accepted commercial practice and for the most part has avoided any major legal challenge. Litigation only seems more likely to arise from an anti-trust or competition law perspective, if periods of exclusivity are too lengthy, a matter considered by the European Commission as it examined a commercial contract executed by the Danish Tennis Federation (DTF) in or around 1998. Ultimately, the Commission approved of the DTF's sponsorship contract with its tennis ball suppliers.[348]

533. Separate and apart from the commercial context of the CPL are the questions of dispute resolution and the governing law. CPL has traditionally used standard clauses in this regard, admirably incorporating the procedural rules of the CAS:

> This Agreement shall be governed by and construed in accordance with the laws of Trinidad and Tobago … All disputes arising out of or in connection

347. *Ibid*, Clause 4.14.
348. 'The Commission conditionally approves sponsorship contracts between the Danish Tennis Federation and its tennis ball suppliers', http://europa.eu/rapid/press-release_IP-98-355_en.htm?locale=en.

with this Agreement shall be referred to and finally resolved by arbitration, *mutatis mutandis*, pursuant to the Procedural Rules of the Court of Arbitration for Sport, (the 'Rules') which Rules are deemed to be incorporated by reference into this Clause.

534. This express incorporation of the procedural rules of the CAS is a legally prudent step in light of the recent decision of the England and Wales High Court in *Bony v. Kacou and others,*[349] where the failure of the defendants to expressly incorporate the arbitration rules of the English Football Association was fatal to its application for a stay of proceedings for the purpose of arbitration.

535. In summary, the legal backdrop of the CPL has given welcome experience to Trinidad and Tobago as an event host.

VII. The ICC Women's T20 World Cup 2018

536. The hosting of cricket events in Trinidad and Tobago was almost extended at the end of 2017 as the ICC awarded the 2018 edition of the T20 Women's World Cup to the West Indies. The only outstanding issue would be which Caribbean territories would share hosting responsibilities.

537. Trinidad and Tobago's ultimate indecision cost it the opportunity to be considered as a host, resulting in some media backlash. There were genuine concerns among local sporting authorities that all of the financial and legal obligations needed to be fully explored before the country could submit a proper bid. In the words of Mr Dinanath Ramnarine, former West Indies spin bowler and the then chairman of the board of SPORTT:

> My understand[ing] is that a bid is going to go but whether they're going to meet all the requirements, I don't know … I don't think that ($1 million) is a fair assessment of the cost. There are many hidden costs, I don't think the TTCB can evaluate that. When you count customs, immigration, taxes, you can only base that by providing numbers. I have not seen that data. I think that $1million is highly conservative, it might be significantly higher. The one cost they would have provided is the US$75,000 that has to be a guarantee as part of the bid. Then they're asking waiver of all taxes, customs (fee), security and so on.[350]

349. [2017] EWHC 2146 (Ch).
350. Stephon Nicholas, *Shaky bid for Women's World Cup*, 8 Dec. 2017, https://newsday.co.tt/2017/12/08/shaky-bid-for-womens-world-cup/

538. Ramnarine's cautious approach, therefore, was based on whether a sufficiently thorough pre-tournament analysis was done in advance of the bid by Trinidad and Tobago to share hosting responsibilities. Ultimately, the hosting rights were awarded to Guyana, Antigua and Barbuda and St. Lucia. This missed opportunity would hopefully offer valuable lessons for the possible hosting of future events.

VIII. The 2021 Commonwealth Youth Games

539. In late 2018, Trinidad and Tobago was one of only two countries to bid for the right to host the 2021 CYG.[351] This follows the successful hosting of the 2017 edition of the CYG by another Caribbean country, the Bahamas. Should Trinidad and Tobago's bid be a successful one, there would be a general sentiment that the country would, by then, have had sufficient experience in understanding the legal and regulatory framework for sports event hosting.

540. If the bidding process for CYG 2021 in any way resembles Olympic bidding then Trinidad and Tobago, like Gibraltar, can expect some form of evaluation to occur under some of the following themes:

- motivation, concept and public opinion;
- political support;
- finance;
- venues;
- accommodation;
- transport infrastructure;
- general conditions, logistics and experience.[352]

541. The legal backdrop to a 2021 bid, though, is not likely to involve the introduction of sui generis ambush marketing legislation since the trend of previous CYG and Youth Olympic Games suggests that such a need is generally disproportionate to the magnitude of the Games. At best, the legal framework for any winning bid will be founded on existing intellectual property laws, especially copyright and trademark, the common law tort of passing off and the use of awareness campaigns that educate stakeholders about branding, marketing, media guidelines and social media use in and around the event.

---

351. 'CGF receive bids from Gibraltar and Trinidad and Tobago for 2021 Commonwealth Youth Games'-Michael Pavitt, 25 Oct. 2018, https://www.insidethegames.biz/articles/1071453/cgf-receive-bids-from-gibraltar-and-trinidad-and-tobago-for-2021-commonwealth-youth-games.

352. 1 Vassil Girginov, *Handbook of the London 2012 Olympic and Paralympic Games* 33 (Routledge 2016).

§3. MEDIA AND TELEVISION RIGHTS

542. The Caribbean is not generally known for generating multimillion dollar sports broadcasting contracts. The reasons are two-fold. First, the small market based on many tiny geographical populations usually means that any given target audience is already limited in size. Second, the sports properties in the region have struggled to attract the size of viewing audience to foster a sustainable industry that is based on Caribbean-centric content. Regional media houses depend on overseas content to maintain and/or expand their viewership.

543. Notwithstanding these challenges, media houses in Trinidad and Tobago such as Flow Sports, DirecTV, CNC 3 and TV 6 have managed to attract local audiences to their coverage of local and international sport. Notably, the court's intervention in sports broadcasting cases has been virtually non-existent in Trinidad and Tobago, so that the recent *Telemundo* decision stands out as a rare case study involving sports broadcasting. This initial ruling was based on a preliminary procedural legal point.

Telemundo Network Group LLC. v. Trinidad and Tobago Football Association.[353]

544. Some of the salient facts of this case, from a legal standpoint, are adequately summarised in paragraphs 10–12 of the judgment of Dean-Armorer J. in the following words:

> In May, 2012, the Trinidad and Tobago Football Association attended the 35th Ordinary Congress of the Caribbean Football Union and accepted a proposal for the bundling of their broadcasting rights and the sale of those rights to a company, Traffic Sports. The acceptance by the Trinidad and Tobago Football Association of the proposal was later notarised in a document dated the 29th August, 2012 and entitled 'Transfer of Broadcast Rights'.
>
> On the 28th August, 2012, Broadcasting Rights were transferred to Traffic Sports under the Rights Acquisition Agreement (the 'Traffic Agreement') which was executed between the Caribbean Football Union and Traffic Sports USA. This agreement was signed by Gordon Dereck, President of the Caribbean Football Union and Aaron Davidson, President of Traffic Sports USA. The governing law of this agreement is the laws of New York [See 'E.V. 6' of the affidavit of Eli Velazquez filed on the 14th March, 2017, at Clause 13].
>
> Lastly, the Soccer License Agreement or the 'Telemundo Agreement' was executed in May, 2015. It was made between Media World, LLC ('Media World'), Traffic Sports USA ('Traffic') and Telemundo. The governing law of the Telemundo Agreement is the law of the State of Florida and with regard to any pre action or litigation, proceedings could only be instituted in the Federal or State Courts within the Miami-Da[d]e County, Florida.

353. CV2017/00898.

545. From the above summary, three legal documents fell due for interpretation:

(1) the Transfer of Broadcast Rights document;
(2) the Rights Acquisition Agreement; and
(3) the Soccer Licence Agreement.

546. Pursuant to the Transfer of Broadcast Rights document, the TTFA bundled together the 2018 FIFA World Cup qualifying broadcast rights and sold those rights to Traffic Sports. The formal transfer of the rights to Traffic Sports took place in accordance with the Rights Acquisition Agreement.

547. One legal challenge that occurred in this case was initiated by an entity known as the Elite Soccer Agency who had allegedly become the beneficiaries of a transfer of the right to broadcast qualifying matches for the 2018 FIFA World Cup in Russia. Telemundo Network Group LLC ('Telemundo') claimed that it, and not Elite Soccer Agency, possessed those broadcast rights. Elite Soccer Agency, in turn, claimed that all contracts executed prior to its receipt of the relevant broadcast rights were invalid.

548. At this juncture of the proceedings, the court addressed the related themes of the appropriateness of both a stay of proceedings and the grant of injunctive relief to the Claimant, Telemundo. However, as it relates to the question of sports media rights, paragraph 37 of the judgment is instructive:

> It was my view, that the claimant has presented a serious question to be tried. The claimant has not relied on the law of contract. Rather, the claimant contends that the defendant has disregarded the rights accruing to the claimant under the chain of contracts and has wrongfully attempted to sell those rights to a third party. Accordingly, the claimant contends, and I accept, Telemundo is entitled to approach the Court under the Protection Against Unfair Competition [Act] 1996 [Protection Against Unfair Competition [Act] 1996, Chapter 82:36].

549. It is noteworthy that the court observed the Claimant' choice not to rely on contract law. Instead, reliance was placed on competition law, enshrined within the Unfair Competition Act.[354] The court agreed with this approach. In the court's view, Telemundo was right to challenge the attempt by the TTFA to transfer broadcast rights to a third party, namely, Elite Soccer Agency.

550. Significantly, this appears to be one of the few times that the Unfair Competition Act has been tested in the courts of Trinidad and Tobago, especially in the context of sport. As short as this statute is, there seems to be great potential for it to

354. Chapter 82:36.

be used as a tool to protect various sports-related rights, including protection against ambush marketing and the unlawful use of a person's image. This latter theme will be developed in the next section.

551. Ultimately, the court granted injunctive relief to the Claimant, with Dean-Armorer J. concluding as follows: 'I will accordingly grant the injunctive relief, in respect of the matches to be aired on the 24th and 28th March, 2017. The qualifying matches for 2020 are scheduled to be heard in the distant future, and there is a great likelihood that the substantive claim would be determined by then'. The court's view was that by the time the qualifying matches for the 2022 FIFA World Cup in Qatar came around, there would have been resolution to the main claim.

552. The *Telemundo* case, although only at the preliminary stage, has the potential to impact the development of future sports broadcasting case law in Trinidad and Tobago and the wider region.

§4. Image Rights and Persona Protection

553. As mentioned in the foregoing section, one of the statutes invoked in the *Telemundo* case was the Unfair Competition Act. Although the legislative drafters are unlikely to have had sports personalities as the focal point of this statute, there is reason for optimism with regards to using this legislation to protect sports rights.

554. The relevant provisions are sections 5–8 of the Act. Section 5 reads, in part, as follows:

> (1) Any act or practice, in the course of industrial or commercial activities, that causes, or is likely to cause, confusion with respect to another's enterprise or its activities, in particular, the products or services offered by such enterprise, shall constitute an act of unfair competition. (2) Confusion may, in particular, be caused with respect to any of the following: (a) a trade mark, whether registered or not; (b) a trade name; (c) a business identifier other than a trade mark or trade name; (d) the appearance of a product; (e) the presentation of products or services; (f) a celebrity or a well-known fictional character.

555. Section 5(1) above uses the language of causing confusion which resembles trademark law, the tort of passing off, ambush marketing protection and depending on the jurisdiction, image rights and persona protection. Specifically, that subsection deems an act of unlawful competition to have taken place if that act or practice causes or is likely to cause confusion with regard to another person's enterprise or activities.

556. For an infringement to occur, the context in which the act must have taken place must be commercial or industrial activities. This is the same legal foundation on which trademark law is based. Further, there must be confusion or the likelihood of confusion with respect to the activities or enterprise of another. It is here that shades of *Fenty v. Arcadia*[355] (the 'Rihanna' case) and *The Robert Marley Foundation v. Dino Michelle*[356] (the 'Bob Marley' case) are found.

557. In both *Rihanna* and *Bob Marley*, the infringing act was the unauthorised use of both celebrities' images on T-shirts being sold by the respective defendants. In both cases, the courts found passing off to have been made out on the facts, with Clarke J. in *Bob Marley* going a step further in also finding the tort of appropriation of personality to have been committed.

558. The court in *Rihanna* was explicit in its conviction that no such thing as image rights existed under English law. It stated that there 'is in English law no "image right" or "character right" which allows a celebrity to control the use of his or her name or image'.[357] It added that a 'celebrity seeking to control the use of his or her image must therefore rely upon some other cause of action such as breach of contract, breach of confidence, infringement of copyright or, as in this case, passing off'.[358]

559. It is worth noting as well that the *Rihanna* decision seemed to turn on the specific evidence adduced in that case and, in particular, the fact that there was a pre-existing relationship between the litigants. In the absence of that relationship, it is unlikely that passing off would have been found to exist.

560. The court in *Bob Marley* equally did not affirm the existence of an image right in Commonwealth Caribbean law but appeared to be more open-minded than the Court of Appeal in *Rihanna*. Clarke J.'s concluding position was this:

> I hold, therefore, that Bob Marley, a celebrity of renown at home and abroad, had a right to the exclusive use of his name and likeness or image. The right entitled him to exploit it commercially. He could, for instance, for a fee, license persons to use his name and likeness etc. for commercial gain. That right survived his death. The plaintiff is the assignee of that right in Jamaica. And as the statement of claim pleads, the plaintiff is invested with the proprietary right in the exclusive marketing for gain in Jamaica of the license to use his image, photograph, name, all indicia of his personality. In my judgment, the commercial use of Bob Marley's name and likeness or image by the defendant without the plaintiff's consent constitutes an invasion or impairment of the plaintiff's exclusive right as aforesaid resulting in damage to the plaintiff. Such conduct on the defendant's part constitutes the tort of appropriation of personality, separate and distinct from the tort of passing off.[359]

355. [2015] EWCA Civ 3.
356. JM 1994 SC 032.
357. 2015] EWCA Civ 3 at para. 29.
358. *Ibid.*, at para. 33.
359. JM 1994 SC 032.

561. Passing off, it is well established will be found if the three core criteria of goodwill, misrepresentation and damage can be established.

562. In summary, on the facts of *Bob Marley*, the court was willing to find that two torts were committed: passing off *and* appropriation of personality. The crucial aspect of this standpoint was Clarke J.'s view that Bob Marley and his assigns had the right to exclusively use and to commercially exploit his name, likeness or image.

563. Returning, then, to the question of confusion, as found in the Unfair Competition Act, it seems that this would accord with the second limb of the passing off criteria, namely, misrepresentation. It suggests, therefore, that a Claimant seeking to rely on section 5(1) of the Unfair Competition Act may feel some security that he or she is not introducing a concept that is foreign to the courts of law.

564. A famous person can take further comfort from section 5(2)(f) which states that confusion may be caused in relation to a celebrity or a well-known fictional character. Yet, to rely successfully on this subsection, the confusion would have to be in a commercial context and must relate to the celebrity's enterprise or activities.

565. This element has similarities with the first limb of the passing off criteria, namely, goodwill.[360] It is why both claimants in *Rihanna* and *Bob Marley* could successfully bring their claims since they both were involved in commercial enterprises by virtue of their respective merchandising practices. This, too, increases the potential for section 5 of the Unfair Competition Act being favourably invoked.

566. This now leaves only the third element of passing off, which is damage. The language of section 6 is lucid. It says:

> (1) Any act or practice, in the course of industrial or commercial activities, that damages, or is likely to damage, the goodwill or reputation of another's enterprise shall constitute an act of unfair competition, regardless of whether such act or practice causes confusion. (2) Damaging another's goodwill or reputation may, in particular, result from the dilution of the goodwill or reputation attached to any of the following: (a) a trade mark, whether registered or not; (b) a trade name; (c) a business identifier other than a trade mark or trade name; (d) the appearance of a product; (e) the presentation of products or services; (f) a celebrity or a well-known fictional character.

567. An act of unfair competition is committed by someone whose action damages or is likely to damage the goodwill or reputation of the Claimant's enterprise. Section 6(2)(f) uses language that is similar to section 5(2)(f) where it speaks to the dilution of the goodwill or reputation of a celebrity.

---

360. The three elements necessary to establish passing off were cited in Reckitt & Colman Products Ltd. V Borden Inc. [1990] All ER 873 (also known as the 'Jif Lemon' case).

568. Sections 7 and 8 prima facie seem to have limited usefulness in protecting sports rights. They state as follows:

7. (1) Any act or practice, in the course of industrial or commercial activities, that misleads, or is likely to mislead, the public with respect to an enterprise or its activities, in particular, the products or services offered by such enterprise, shall constitute an act of unfair competition. (2) Misleading may arise out of advertising or promotion and may, in particular, occur with respect to any of the following: (a) the manufacturing process of a product; (b) the suitability of a product or service for a particular purpose; (c) the quality or quantity or other characteristics of products or services; (d) the geographical origin of products or services; (e) the conditions on which products or services are offered or provided; (f) the price of products or services or the manner in which it is calculated.
8. (1) Any false or unjustifiable allegation, in the course of industrial or commercial activities, that discredits, or is likely to discredit, another's enterprise or its activities, in particular, the products or services offered by such enterprise, shall constitute an act of unfair competition. (2) Discrediting may arise out of advertising or promotion and may, in particular, occur with respect to any of the following: (a) the manufacturing process of a product; (b) the suitability of a product or service for a particular purpose; (c) the quality or quantity or other characteristics of products or services; (d) the conditions on which products or services are offered or provided; (e) the price of products or services or the manner in which it is calculated.

569. These sections speak to conduct that misleads or is likely to mislead (section 7) or discredits or is likely to discredit (section 8). Admittedly, though, the misleading or discrediting activity is more connected to the quality, price, suitability or geographic origin of a product or service. The legislation does not appear to be aimed at outlawing commercial affiliations with another's products or services. Reliance on these sections, then, for the purposes of sports rights protection is unlikely to bring success.

570. It is unfortunate that the Unfair Competition Act has not really been tested in a sporting context in the courts of Trinidad and Tobago as judicial pronouncements would significantly chart the future direction of this statute whether towards or away from sports rights protection, including image rights. Perhaps the apparent overlap created between the provisions of the Unfair Competition Act, trademark law and passing off has, to some degree, negated much reliance on the statutory framework. The groundwork, it is submitted, is already set for the Unfair Competition Act to take its place in shaping the future of sports law in Trinidad and Tobago.

§5. Merchandising

571. One of the laments among sports stakeholders in Trinidad and Tobago is the general inability to purchase locally made sports merchandise. The sobering reality, from a sports marketing perspective, is that in Trinidad and Tobago you are more likely to find fans wearing the jerseys of football clubs like Barcelona, Real Madrid, Bayern Munich, Juventus, AC Milan, Chelsea, Arsenal, Liverpool, Manchester City and Manchester United. Other than club jerseys, it is also commonplace to find on the backs of adults and children alike, certain national team kits such as those from Brazil, Argentina, Germany and France, in particular.

572. The same zeal does not exist for local club teams, although there is a real chance of finding fans wearing the football jerseys of their former schools. It is only during a FIFA World Cup qualifying campaign that local fans will proudly wear the national team's jersey but local club jerseys are quite scarce.

573. This scenario, therefore, has left a merchandising void in Trinidad and Tobago. This seems to be directly connected to the value that is placed on the local sporting product. That value is itself inextricably linked to the success of the team in question. It is for this reason that one of the more popular sports kits in the country is that of the Trinbago [361] Knight Riders (TKR), the franchise T20 cricket team whose core players are from Trinidad and Tobago.

574. Jersey sales have tended to rise around the time of the annual CPL and local sales were boosted both in 2017 and 2018 when TKR won back-to-back titles. The fact of TKR being the defending champions by the time the 2019 edition of the tournament comes around will be an added fillip to T-shirt sales even before the event begins. However, it will take a radical turnaround in the local sports marketing landscape over time, before a sustainable merchandising business can be established.

§6. Conclusion

575. In light of the foregoing, the hosting of sporting events in Trinidad and Tobago appears to have a bright future. Its tropical weather, festive culture and penchant for leisure make it a wonderful host of athletes and spectators alike. Yet, there is quite a lot of untapped potential in this twin-island which needs to be extracted and expressed if Trinidad and Tobago is going to be a respected stakeholder in the family of sport.

361. 'Trinbago' is a commonly used abbreviation referring to the country Trinidad and Tobago.

576. Arguably, those who consume sport in Trinidad and Tobago as well as those who regulate it have become more legally savvy and, generally, more knowledgeable of the key considerations that impact on the successful organisation and delivery of sports events. While a senior FIFA World Cup or Olympic bid might still be ambitious, there is little or nothing to prevent this country from setting its sights on the future hosting of elite events.

577. Additionally, the sports tourism industry seems well placed to be a catalyst that helps that transition from possibility to actuality, as is the intellectual property industry. The vision for the future of the business of sport is succinctly captured in the 2017–2027 NSP of Trinidad and Tobago: 'To establish the sporting industry as a viable candidate for economic diversification, by capitalizing and maximizing revenue generating potential and capabilities.'[362] It is important for the sustainability of the industry that the decision-makers keep their eye on that vision.

362. Article 14.9, p. 37.

Chapter 3. The Commercial Integrity of Sport

§1. Introduction

578. There is general agreement that the phenomenal growth of the business of sport has brought with it, both the capacity for great income-earning potential, but also the threat of corrupt or unethical practices. Sport in Trinidad and Tobago is no exception and has had to face its own integrity challenges at various levels.

§2. Football Finances and Accountability: The David Simmons Report

579. In or around the year 2015, FIFA introduced a Club Licensing System to its members among the respective confederations including CONCACAF. FIFA itself succinctly summed up the objective of the Club Licensing System by noting that the programme was 'based on five key criteria: sporting, personnel and administrative, financial, infrastructure and legal. These criteria aim to safeguard the credibility and integrity of club competitions while improving the level of professionalism within the football family and promoting transparency in the finances, ownership and control of clubs'.[363]

580. Yet, these noble goals of credibility, integrity and transparency would be tested on a larger scale through the fires of legal scrutiny mere months after this FIFA announcement, when the 2015 FIFA Congress became the incredible scene of arrests and downright shock as Swiss law enforcement authorities descended on the Baur au Lac hotel in May of that year. It would not be the first time that the football family would be called to account for its governance.

I. The David Simmons Report into Football Fraud

581. The Executive Summary of the 2013 CONCACAF Integrity Committee Report of Investigation told a sobering story of poor football governance in the Caribbean with particular emphasis on activities occurring in Trinidad and Tobago. The Committee noted, in part, as follows:

> The Committee concluded that Jack Warner committed fraud against CONCACAF and FIFA in connection with the COE[364] in two ways. First, Warner secured funds from FIFA and CONCACAF by falsely representing, and intentionally creating a false impression, that the land on which the COE was developed was owned by CONCACAF when he knew that it was in fact owned by his own companies. Second, Warner induced FIFA to transfer funds that were

363. *FIFA and CONCACAF Introduce Club Licensing in the CONCACAF Region*, 15 Jan. 2015, https://www.fifa.com/governance/news/y=2015/m=1/news=fifa-and-concacaf-introduce-club-licensing-in-the-concacaf-region-2507080.html.

364. Centre of Excellence.

intended for development of the COE to himself personally by falsely representing that bank accounts to which FIFA should send the funds were CONCACAF accounts when he knew that in fact he controlled them personally. The Committee also concluded that Warner committed fraud and misappropriated funds that were sent by Football Federation Australia ('FFA') to CONCACAF for development of the COE, and that he breached his fiduciary duties to CONCACAF through fraud and misappropriation of funds. The Committee further concluded that Warner violated the CONCACAF Statutes by arranging for others to sign loan guarantees related to the COE on behalf of CONCACAF without obtaining approval from the Congress, and that Warner violated the FIFA Ethics Code by engaging in self-dealing through fraud and misappropriation.[365]

582. Similar findings were made in relation to the late American Charles 'Chuck' Blazer who at the time served as CONCACAF's Secretary General. Both Blazer and Warner would find themselves again under close legal scrutiny following the 2015 arrests of FIFA officials in Switzerland. Sadly, Blazer died in July 2017. Warner, on the other hand has been staving off extradition to the USA since that time.

583. The magnitude of the findings against Warner were epitomised by the legal controversy surrounding the ownership of the Centre of Excellence as well as the nebulous operations of CONCACAF in Trinidad and Tobago.

II. The Centre of Excellence: The Question of True Legal Ownership

584. Were it not for media reports around the middle of 2012, the question of the true legal ownership of the Centre of Excellence (COE) may have remained a well-kept secret. As noted in the Simmons Report, the title deeds to the land on which the COE was developed showed that the COE was situated on three distinct parcels of land at Macoya in the Ward of Tacarigua in Trinidad and Tobago.[366] What subsequently was discovered through the work of CONCACAF's Integrity Committee was the fact that each of the three parcels of land was owned by a company controlled by Jack Warner.[367]

585. It was further established through the evidence gathered that funds provided by FIFA to CONCACAF were used to purchase at least one of the plots of land on which the COE was constructed.[368] In fact, the Committee held the view that the timelines of the land purchases and multiple FIFA transfers left the strong

365. *Executive Summary, CONCACAF Integrity Committee Report of Investigation*, 18 April 2013 at p. vi.
366. *Ibid.*, at 22.
367. Renraw Investment Ltd and CCAM and Company Limited.
368. CONCACAF Report, *supra*, n. 366 at 30.

possibility that the FIFA funds were actually used to purchase all three parcels of land.[369] The Simmons Report further highlighted that Warner had myriad occasions to disclose that the properties were purchased by his companies but failed to do so.

586. The impropriety continued when Warner and his companies used the COE property as security for bank loans, with CONCACAF being named as a borrower on the mortgage deed.[370] To add further context, these misdeeds were not easily spotted due to the fact that back in 1996 Warner and his CCAM company registered a partnership in Trinidad and Tobago under the name 'CONCACAF Centre of Excellence' whose aim was to engage in the sport development business.[371] The partnership's name was subsequently changed to the 'Dr Joao Havelange Centre of Excellence'. The Committee indicated that it found no evidence to suggest that the existence of the partnership was ever disclosed to CONCACAF's Executive Committee or Congress or that the use of the CONCACAF name by Warner was ever approved.[372] The Simmons Report also indicated that Warner comingled his personal funds with money donated by the FFA through its International Football Development Programme in connection with its 2022 FIFA World Cup bid.[373]

587. In the midst of this conspicuous disregard for the laws of Florida, New York[374] and Trinidad and Tobago was also a violation of the Statutes of CONCACAF with regard to seeking approval for loans. The applicable provision back then was Article 20(h) of the 1994 Statutes which stipulated that the Congress had to approve the purchase of real property. Article 20(g) stipulated that the Congress also had to authorise loan applications. A combination of Articles 20 and 22 of the 2016 edition of the CONCACAF Statutes grants the current CONCACAF Congress similar authority.

III. CONCACAF's Operations in Trinidad and Tobago

588. The main observation of the Integrity Committee in relation to CONCACAF's operations in Trinidad and Tobago was that all accounting records related to the expenditures at the COE and at the Office of the CONCACAF President seemed to have been created and maintained in Trinidad and Tobago under Warner's control.[375] This occurred notwithstanding the fact that at the material time, CONCACAF's headquarters were located in New York. The Committee further noted that

369. *Ibid.*, p. 31.
370. *Ibid.*, p. 32.
371. *Ibid.*, p. 25.
372. *Ibid.*
373. *Ibid.*, pp. 29–30.
374. CONCACAF's headquarters were originally in New York before they moved it to Miami. In November 2018, CONCACAF opened new headquarters also in Miami. *See* '*Infantino: New CONCACAF HQ represents new chapter of football in the region.*' 19 Nov. 2018, https://www.concacaf.com/en/article/infantino-new-concacaf-hq-represents-new-chapter-of-football-in-region.
375. CONCACAF Report, *supra*, n. 366 at 40.

CONCACAF had failed to include the financial activity of its operations in Trinidad and Tobago in its general accounting ledgers.[376]

IV. Comment

589. The publication of the CONCACAF Report and its findings was a reminder that the preservation of ethical practices and sporting integrity in football was not axiomatic. The fact that there was compelling evidence against officials in high places would have damaged CONCACAF's credibility. In fact, this concern was identified at paragraph 2.1 of the Report: 'Allegations of corruption and self-dealing have the obvious potential to impair CONCACAF's reputation for integrity. CONCACAF's reputation for integrity is vital to its effectiveness and success in light of its role in governing and administering football as well as its role in sponsoring major public tournaments.'[377]

590. Allegations associated with the conduct of Jack Warner would eventually become part and parcel of two cases heard at the CAS. In *Mohamed Bin Hammam v. FIFA*,[378] the CAS panel in finding that the charges of corruption against Bin Hammam were not made out made the following concluding remarks:

> The Panel wishes to make clear that this conclusion should not be taken to diminish the significance of its finding that it is more likely than not that Mr. Bin Hammam was the source of the monies that were brought into Trinidad and Tobago and eventually distributed at the meeting by Mr. Warner, and that in this way, his conduct, in collaboration with and most likely induced by Mr. Warner, may not have complied with the highest ethical standards that should govern the world of football and other sports. This is all the more so at the elevated levels of football governance at which individuals such as Mr. Bin Hammam and Mr. Warner have operated in the past.[379]

591. The panel raised concerns about how both Bin Hammam and Warner conducted themselves as high-ranking football officials. More recently in *Jerome Valcke v. FIFA*,[380] the CAS panel had to decide upon two related questions, namely, '(i) from a factual standpoint, whether the Appellant with this email to Mr Warner actually "offered" or "attempted to offer" the CFU an undue benefit or only "expressed his intent" to take the matter to the Marketing and TV Board Committee, and (ii) if so, what are the legal consequences of that offer'.[381]

376. *Ibid.*, at 41.
377. *Ibid.*, at 9.
378. CAS 2011/A/2625.
379. *Ibid.*, at para. 204.
380. CAS 2017/A/5003.
381. *Ibid.*, at para. 242.

592. The concern in this case, *inter alia*, was whether email communication between Valcke and Warner constituted an offer to the Caribbean Football Union, over which Warner presided, of an undue benefit with respect to the grant of broadcasting rights contrary to the FIFA COE. The growing chain of allegations against Warner over a period of six to seven years left serious doubt over the propriety of his leadership tenure while he served as a football administrator. Additionally, a cloud has also been left over the proper legal ownership of the Joao Havelange Centre of Excellence in Trinidad and Tobago arising from the allegations made against Warner in the David Simmons Report.

§3. Football Finances and Accountability: The TTFA

593. The TTFA has consistently been named as a Defendant in the Supreme Court of Justice in Trinidad and Tobago raising questions as to whether sufficient reforms have been made to its governance and commercial practices. Regular challenges to the leadership of the extant TTFA Executive Committee have caused stakeholders to assess whether true change has occurred since the Warner era.

594. One of the matters ventilated before the local courts involved the call for financial accountability of the TTFA. In *Charles et al v. The Trinidad and Tobago Football Association and Oliver Camps*,[382] the Claimant footballers who represented Trinidad and Tobago at the 2006 FIFA World Cup in Germany, sought various reliefs against the TTFA. These reliefs included:

(1) an account of all the money due from the TTFA to the footballers under an agreement made at various meetings between 2005 and 2006;
(2) an account of all the money paid to the Second Defendant, who was the former TTFA President;
(3) payment of USD 26,608.70, representing a Charity Withheld Sum;
(4) payment of CHF 755,550, representing a Tax/Insurance Withheld Sum;
(5) an order for payment by the TTFA and/or the Second Defendant of all monies due and owing to the footballers; and
(6) Damages for breach of contract.

595. Rampersad J. in this case examined the law of agency in view of the fact Jack Warner, the then Special Adviser to the TTFA, was seen by many to be the person with de facto control of the organisation. The application to join Warner as a defendant pursuant to Part 19 of the 2005 Civil Proceedings Rules was ultimately rejected. Citing Halsbury's Laws of England,[383] the court noted:

382. Claim No. CV2007-02238.
383. Halsbury's Laws of England/AGENCY (VOLUME 1 (2008) 5TH EDITION)/7. RELATIONS BETWEEN AGENT AND THIRD PERSONS/(1) LIABILITIES OF AGENT/(iii) Money Received by Agent/162. Liability to repay to third person.

> *The receipt of money from a third person by an agent on his principal's behalf does not in itself render the agent personally liable to repay it when the third person becomes entitled as against the principal to repayment, whether the money remains in the agent's hands or not. If, however, a third person pays money to an agent under a mistake of fact, or in consequence of some wrongful act, the agent is personally liable to repay unless, before the claim for repayment was made upon him, he has paid it to the principal or done something equivalent to payment to his principal, or where the principal is a foreign sovereign immune from suit. Where, however, the agent has been a party to the wrongful act, or has acted as a principal in the transaction, in consequence of which the money has been paid to him, he is not discharged from his liability to make repayment by any payment over to his principal.*[384] [Emphasis original]

596. Rampersad J. was clear to state that the footballers made no claim during the case for Warner to repay them but he saw it important to articulate that 'this exposition of the law demonstrates where and to whom the duty to account lies in relation to monies received by an agent'.[385]

597. Warner's verbal promise to the 2006 World Cup footballers was the catalyst for this and the previously discussed related claim between the same parties, in which the TTFA sought a stay of proceedings pursuant to the Arbitration Act[386] of Trinidad and Tobago.[387]

598. Still, the issue of proper financial accounting has seemed to plague the TTFA, with the High Court recently ruling against the local football governing body on 13 December 2018. In *Jerwyn Balthazar and others v. Trinidad and Tobago Football Association*[388] the Claimants comprised the players and support staff of the national futsal[389] team, with their claim against the TTFA including an alleged breach of contract arising from the non-payment of over TTD 300,000 (approx. USD 40,000.) in stipends.

599. The case turned on the question as to whether there was a valid and binding oral contract between the players and a past TTFA President, a matter which was eventually decided in the footballers' favour. The existence of this binding oral agreement meant that the TTFA was in breach by not paying the relevant stipends. Unfortunately, the alleged non-payment of salaries, match fees, stipends and

384. Claim No. CV2007-02238, p. 6.
385. *Ibid.*
386. Chapter 5:01 of the Laws of Trinidad and Tobago.
387. *See* the discussion of this case in Ch. 3 of Part I of this book at para. 232 et seq.
388. Claim No. CV2017-04051.
389. Futsal is a specialised form of indoor football played in accordance with the FIFA Futsal Laws of the Game.

bonuses has become a trend in the TTFA's administration of local football in recent years resulting either in actual litigation, the threat of it or player boycotts.[390]

600. The court in *Balthazar v. TTFA* was scathing in its rebuke of the governing body:

> In my opinion it was disingenuous for the Defendant to adopt the position it took with respect [to] the payment of the monthly stipends, per diem and match fees to the Technical Staff and the players respectively since based on the Defendant's conduct it actively le[d] the Claimants to believe that nothing had changed and that the Defendant would have honoured the oral agreement made by Mr. Tim Kee on behalf of the Defendant with the Claimants.
>
> I have concluded that the Claimants provided credible evidence to demonstrate that the Defendant agreed to pay the Technical Staff the monthly stipends which they pleaded and the per diem allowances. The Defendants failed to pay all the sums claimed without any basis for doing so. The Claimants who were players also provided credible evidence that the Defendant agreed to pay certain sums as pleaded as per diem and match fees and the Defendant failed to honour the terms of the said agreement to pay them all the said sums.[391]

601. This ruling serves as a reminder of the gulf that currently exists between the administration of local football and sports governance best practice.

§4. The Life Sport Controversy

602. One of the biggest controversies to impact the Trinidad and Tobago sports fraternity was the scandal that simply became known as 'Life Sport'. The fallout from this debacle included the resignation of a Government Minister.[392] Life Sport's objective was an admirable one as it sought to offer opportunities for 'at risk' youths in the country to better themselves through the avenue of sport. Unfortunately, the noble intentions were subsumed by questionable financial management of the programme.

603. One of the products from Life Sport was the compilation of a 143-page report from the CAC of the Ministry of Finance. The report enumerated the following conclusions:

- there were widespread breaches of procurement practices;
- the approval given by Cabinet was not strictly adhered to;

390. 'TTFA pays four match fees but Warriors maintain strike threat; DJW urged to reveal contracts with foreign FAs', 24 Dec. 2018, https://wired868.com/2018/12/24/ttfa-pays-two-match-fees-but-warriors-maintain-strike-threat-djw-urged-to-reveal-contracts-with-foreign-fas/.
391. Jerwyn Balthazar and others v TTFA-Claim No. CV2017-04051 at paras 138 and 139.
392. Reshma Ragoonath, *After Mounting Calls, Anil Quits*, Trinidad Guardian, 31 Jul. 2014, http://www.guardian.co.tt/article-6.2.385863.1b9ccc2046.

- persons at the coordinating level may have been involved in criminal activity;
- there were several instances of fraudulent activity by suppliers to the Programme;
- there may have been widespread theft of equipment from the Programme;
- there may have been breaches of the Proceeds of Crime Act;
- exorbitant and questionable payments were made in several instances; and
- there was poor control and monitoring of the Programme by the Ministry of Sport.[393]

604. The findings of the report were sufficiently grave that a recommendation was made for the intervention of the Director of Public Prosecutions. The report stated as follows: 'Given the widespread nature of the breaches, it is difficult to understand how they went unnoticed by the Ministry of Sport. Consideration has to be given to whether there was complicity by officers of the Ministry. For example, the entire payment of $34 m to EBeam Interact Limited was made notwithstanding that external attorneys advised that there may have been grounds to contest and resist the final payment.'[394] It further recommended 'that the entire matter be turned over to the Director of Public Prosecution and the Commissioner of Police to prosecute the several breaches identified'.[395]

605. At the time of writing no arrests related to Life Sport were reported although the sitting Government representatives have asserted that the matter has not gone into abeyance.

606. Interestingly, the very CAC (CAC) that penned the Life Sport report was sued in the Trinidad and Tobago High Court by the former Permanent Secretary at the Ministry of Sport. In *Creed et al v. Central Audit Committee*,[396] Dean-Armorer J. ruled, inter alia, that the CAC breached the Claimant Permanent Secretary's legitimate expectation in not affording him an opportunity to be heard when the report was being compiled. As a result, the court ruled that the report should be quashed and remitted to the CAC.

607. The Life Sport litigation, then, was centred on procedural fairness and settled principles of administrative law rather than on the propriety of the conduct of those managing public money. In this light, the 2015 Public Procurement and Disposal of Public Property Act[397] would have been introduced to the local legal system at an opportune time, providing a regulatory basis for the handling of state funds being used for sporting purposes.

393. *Final Report of the Central Audit Committee on the Comprehensive Audit of the Payment System of the Lifesport Programme*, 25 Jul. 2014, p. 4.
394. *Ibid.*
395. *Ibid.*
396. TT 2016 HC 230.
397. Act No 1 of 2015.

§5. Winning at Any Cost: The SSFL

608.

> I need, as President of the League, to have a serious discussion with schools and coaches about how the actions we are taking are affecting the survival of the League in terms of our sponsors[398]

609. The year 2017 was an unforgettable year for schoolboy football in Trinidad and Tobago, but unfortunately for all the wrong reasons. The above lament of William Wallace, the President of the SSFL of Trinidad and Tobago came on the heels of a turbulent season plagued by numerous off-the-field protests and the intervention of the Fraud Squad.

610. Besides Wallace's concerns about the SSFL's integrity and reputation, he also brought to the fore the potentially devastating commercial impact the 2017 scandal could have had on the League. His anxiety about whether the SSFL's sponsors would consider withdrawing future financial investment was a legitimate one, even though this was only a league for student-athletes.

611. The most conspicuous feature of the 2017 SSFL Premiership season was the expulsion of a school by the name of Fyzabad Secondary School ('Fyzabad'), one of sixteen teams[399] to participate in that season's round-robin tournament. The reason for Fyzabad's suspension was its falsification of the academic certificates of two of its players to facilitate their participation in the 2017 season.[400]

612. Both the players and the team manager of Fyzabad sought to lay blame on each other, but the initial deduction of points culminated in their eventual suspension from the league. The school's principal subsequently removed all of his school teams from the various competitions in which they were involved that year.[401] The intervention of the Fraud Squad attached to the Trinidad and Tobago Police Service would have confirmed the gravity of the situation to onlookers.[402]

---

398. *St. Anthony's Go Top After Shiva Boys Protest; Wallace 'Uncomfortable' About SSFL's Direction*, 25 Oct. 2017, https://wired868.com/2017/10/25/st-anthonys-go-top-after-shiva-boys-protest-wallace-uncomfortable-about-ssfls-direction/.
399. The SSFL Premiership tournament started in 2014 and is usually a 15-team tournament. Exceptionally, the 2017 had 16 participating teams but that reverted to 15 teams in 2018.
400. *SSFL Dumps Fyzabad! 'Fyzo Tigers' Suspended for 'Fraudulent' Exam Documents*, 19 Oct. 2017, https://wired868.com/2017/10/19/ssfl-dumps-fyzabad-fyzo-tigers-suspended-for-fraudulent-exam-documents/.
401. *Source: Fyzabad Principal was Deceived Too; School Stops All Football Programmes After Scandal*, 20 Oct. 2017, https://wired868.com/2017/10/20/source-fyzabad-principal-was-deceived-too-school-stops-all-football-programmes-after-scandal/.
402. *Fraud Squad Moves on Fyzabad Forgery: Grills Staff, Players and SSFL Officials*, 27 Oct. 2017, https://wired868.com/2017/10/27/fraud-squad-moves-on-fyzabad-secondary-fraud-police-grill-staff-players-and-ssfl-officials/.

613. Perhaps even more sobering would have been the fact that this intervention actually led to criminal charges being laid against the school principal and the PE teacher. The charges against the principal included four counts of misbehaviour in public office plus two counts of uttering forged CXC[403] certificates. The PE teacher's six charges were similar in nature and included two counts of forgery.[404]

614. The entire scenario, predictably led to closer scrutiny being placed not only on the schools participating in the SSFL but also on the League itself. Reputational damage was a sure consequence of the Fyzabad scandal but it led to deeper questions being asked about the integrity of the sport in general.

615. An onlooker who chose to remain anonymous, made some useful recommendations in the aftermath of the scandal. One suggestion of note was the proposal that the SSFL Executive could be seconded so that they could be elevated from the volunteer status that characterises so much of the administration of sport in Trinidad and Tobago.[405] The proposer systematically identified a clear function for each of the Ministry of Education, the SSFL and the TTFA. In suggesting harsher penalties for infringers as well as FIFA-assisted training and educational initiatives for SSFL administrators, the proposer has continued a much-needed conversation about integrity in governance generally, with direct or indirect implications for commercial integrity specifically.[406]

616. There were no reported cases of sponsor pullouts after the Fyzabad controversy but such a reaction would not have been farfetched. This raises the related question of the commercial viability of the League, a matter which surfaced during the various off-field controversies in 2017.

I. The SSFL as a Commercial Product

617. The drafters of the SSFL constitution evidently contemplated that there was commercial value attached to the Premiership Division comprising the top fifteen football schools across Trinidad and Tobago. An 'Exclusive Rights' clause in the following terms has been included at section 24 of the SSFL constitution: 'The Secondary Schools Football League and its member Schools own the exclusive rights to broadcasts and transmissions of events coming under their jurisdiction via any audio-visual and sound broadcasting media whatsoever, whether live, deferred or excerpts.'

---

403. Caribbean Examinations Council.
404. *Fyzabad Principal and PE Teacher Charged with Six Counts of Fraud Each Over SSFL Scandal*, 16 Nov. 2017, https://wired868.com/2017/11/16/jebodhsingh-and-lakhan-charged-with-six-counts-of-fraud-each-over-ssfl-scandal/.
405. *Dear Editor: The Fyzabad Effect: An SSFL Insider Suggests How to Clean Up the League*, 30 Oct. 2017, https://wired868.com/2017/10/30/dear-editor-the-fyzabad-effect-a-ssfl-insider-suggests-how-to-clean-up-the-league/.
406. *Ibid.*

618. Although not a complex clause, the SSFL envisioned the live or delayed broadcast of its matches with the confidence for this vision, likely arising from its agreement with Digicel and Digicel SportsMax, the latter being one of the leading sports broadcasting organisations in the Caribbean. The five-year USD 1.5 million deal which was signed in November 2015 is a miniscule piece of the global sports media commercial landscape but it was nonetheless a watershed moment for local sports. Match coverage was not limited to the Caribbean but extended to the USA, Canada and the UK.[407]

619. The appeal of the exposure generated by live sports broadcasts was identified as a key consideration in the aftermath of the turbulent 2017 season. In reporting on a stakeholder forum in early 2018, *Wired868* succinctly summed up the dilemma of student-athletes who could potentially earn income instead by playing club football: 'Almost inevitably, though, there will be conflict this September when schoolboys are faced with the choice of playing in front of hundreds of schoolmates and live on SportsMax, or in front of a few dozen onlookers in the Pro League.'[408]

620. Unlike in the USA, student footballers actually have the option to play for a club team, even while registered as a school student as long as the timelines and procedural requirements are met. Article 16(4) (a) and (b) of the SSFL Constitution states that:

> A player, who having been registered and/or is playing with the TTFF or with another League or Association affiliated to the TTFA after 31st August of the current year shall not be eligible to be registered as a player for their school unless they meet the criteria of the Credentials Committee.
>
> (b)Any registered player/s of the League who registers and/ or plays with the TTFA or with another League or Association affiliated to the TTFA, shall immediately lose their registration with the League for the remainder of the season.

621. In other words, the door remains open for a school footballer to play professional or semi-professional football up until August 31st in any given year, if he wishes to play for his school that year.[409] After that date, if he is registered, for instance, with the TT Pro League or the TT Super League, he cannot then play for his school team unless the Credentials Committee of the SSFL approves his registration application.

---

407. Jelani Beckles, *Digicel Signs US$1.5 Million Deal with SSFL*, 15 Nov. 2018, http://www.guardian.co.tt/article-6.2.371736.c27db8ae20.

408. *SSFL Forum: Schools' League Grapples with Issues of Registration, Player Development and TTFA Relations*, 26 Feb. 2018, https://wired868.com/2018/02/26/ssfl-forum-schoolboys-league-grapple-issues-registration-player-development-ttfa-relations/.

409. The SSFL season starts in September every year.

622. The challenge is that the professional league matches are poorly attended and are not a part of the SportsMax broadcasting contract, so that while a small salary can be earned, there is little exposure for the club footballer. A choice to play for one's school brings no remuneration but guarantees regional and international exposure, with its attendant scouting opportunities which can culminate in an overseas professional contract.

623. This situation is in sharp contrast to what obtains under US common law. In *Burrows and others v. Ohio High School Athletic Association*,[410] the plaintiff footballers[411] asserted three causes of action:

(1) an infringement of their rights of association under the free speech clause of the first amendment to the US constitution;
(2) the denial of equal protection of the law and due process of law under the fourteenth amendment to the Constitution; and
(3) that the Defendant's by-laws, if enforced as amended, violate the supremacy clause, Article VI, Clause 2 of the Constitution in that the by-laws created an obstacle to the accomplishment of the congressional intent expressed in the 1978 Amateur Sports Act.[412]

624. The factual background to the case is adequately summarised in paragraph 8 of the judgment as follows:

> During October 1987, OHSAA[413] adopted an amendment to its by-laws, to become effective on the first day of January 1988 and thereafter, which foreclosed appellate students from eligibility to compete in interscholastic high school soccer as members of their respective high schools' teams if they had participated as a member of an independent team including appellate Miami Valley Youth Soccer Association during spring competitions in 1988 and thereafter. A similar regulation applied to all 'team-oriented' sports such as football and basketball, but not to such 'individual' sports as golf, tennis, track and field and swimming. OHSAA rationalized that the bylaw amendments would (1) prevent unfair development of 'power squads' which resulted from team members who played together throughout the entire year as a team at the expense of those high school teams whose players were unable to participate in independent league soccer as a result of geographic, economic, or organizational obstacles; (2) encourage student athletes to participate in a diversity of sports.

625. In short, the Ohio High School Athletic Association (OHSAA), by its amended by-law, prevented students who had played football independently, that is to say, the equivalent to club football, from playing for their schools in the

410. 891 F2d 122 57 Ed. Law Rep. 749.
411. Soccer players in the US.
412. 891 F2d 122 57 Ed. Law Rep. 749.
413. The Ohio High School Athletic Association.

approaching football season. Their justification was that they wished to maintain sporting equilibrium and so discourage the development of the so-called power squads. The school footballers eventually conceded that they had no constitutional right to participate in interscholastic soccer. The court ultimately ruled in favour of the OHSAA. The US courts adopted a similar approach in *Letendre v. Missouri State High School Activities Association.*[414] Mitten summarised the *Letendre* decision noting that 'the court upheld the Missouri State High School Activities' Association's ("MSHSAA") outside competition rule and ruled that it did not violate student-athletes' equal protection rights'.[415]

626. It is hard to conclude that the SSFL constitution was drafted in consideration of the American legal context. It is more likely that the commercial reality of Caribbean sports simply warranted a more liberal approach to income earning and as a result, there was no prohibition on schoolboy footballers playing professionally or semi-professionally just before the start of the SSFL season, once they did not breach the eligibility rules.

§6. Sports Betting

627. The Gambling (Gaming and Betting) Control Bill, 2016 of Trinidad and Tobago defines betting as the 'making or accepting, on a fixed odds or pool betting basis, a bet on the outcome of an animal race, including a horse or dog race, or a sporting event'.[416] It further defines the term 'sports betting' to mean 'all betting on sports events wherever held'.[417] Additionally, 'sport' itself is defined as 'an athletic activity requiring skill or physical prowess and often of a competitive nature'.[418]

628. These definitions reflect the increasing awareness of the existence, if not prevalence of betting in sport in Trinidad and Tobago, especially against the backdrop of the absence of definitions for 'sport' and 'sports betting' in the 1963 Gambling and Betting Act. Still, outside of horse racing, it appears that not much formal oversight is accorded to sports betting, meaning that it is difficult to indicate with certainty, the magnitude of the practice.

629. From a legislative standpoint, only the outdated 1933 Boxing Control Act[419] seems to have contemplated betting in sport, with a brief mention in the Schedule to the Act. Section 24 of Part 1 to the Schedule states: 'No betting shall take place during the progress of any boxing contest and any member of the Board may request the removal of any person offending in this manner and his request must be complied with by the promoter of the contest.' It would be surprising,

414. 86 S.W. 3d 63 (2002).
415. Matthew Mitten, *Sports Law in the United States* 91 (Wolters Kluwer Law & Business 2d ed. 2014)
416. Section 4.
417. *Ibid.*
418. *Ibid.*
419. Chapter 21:52.

though not impossible, if a record could be found of a person having been removed from a boxing contest for having contravened this provision.

630. It is anticipated, though, that when the 2016 Gambling Control Bill is passed into law, more stringent regulation of sports betting in general will be introduced.

§7. Conclusion

631. The pursuit of commercial integrity in sport in Trinidad and Tobago is not an elusive goal. There is sufficient goodwill among stakeholders to ensure that the regulatory system is constantly being strengthened. The need of the hour, however, may be legislative intervention that will serve a proactive and not a reactive function, especially in areas like sports betting which remains largely unregulated. The introduction of a Sports Integrity Act, for instance, would be a welcome initiative by the Parliament of Trinidad and Tobago. Although the Indian Prevention of Sporting Fraud Bill 2013 did not materialise,[420] it was a commendable attempt to offer statutory backing to the efforts of regulators. Trinidad and Tobago should not hesitate to follow that path.

420. *Government Shelves Sports Fraud Bill*, The Tribune, 2 Jun. 2017, https://www.tribuneindia.com/news/sport/government-shelves-sports-fraud-bill/416408.html.

Selected Bibliography

Barker, K. & H. Stevens *Club Law Manual*. 2nd ed. Wildy, Simmonds & Hill Publishing, 2011.

Beloff, M. et al., *Sports Law*. 2nd ed. Hart Publishing, 2012.

Berry, D. *Caribbean Integration Law*. Oxford, 2014.

Blackshaw, I. *International Sports Law: An Introductory Guide*. The Hague, The Netherlands: Asser Press, 2017.

Blackshaw, I. *Sport, Mediation and Arbitration*. T.M.C. Asser Press, 2009.

Champion Jr., W. *Sports Law in a Nutshell*. 5th ed. West Academic Publishing, 2017.

Corthésy, N. & C. Harris-Roper. *Commonwealth Caribbean Employment and Labour Law*. Routledge, 2014.

Foster K. *Is There a Global Sports Law? Lex Sportiva: What is Sports Law?* Robert C.R. Siekmann, Janwillem Soek. Springer, 2012.

Gardiner, S. et al., *Sports Law*. 4th ed. Routledge, 2011.

Ince, B. *Trinidad and Tobago at the Olympic Games: From Rodney Wilkes to George Bovell III*. RPL(1991)LTD, 2005, 17.

James, M. *Sports Law*. 3rd ed. Palgrave Law Masters, 2017, 3.

Johnson, P. *Ambush Marketing: A Practical Guide to Protecting the Brand of a Sporting Event*. EIPR Practice Series, Book 1. Thomson, Sweet & Maxwell, 2007.

Koo, J. Full Blown Entertainment: A Missed Opportunity for Advancing the Copyright Law of Developing Commonwealth Countries with Hybrid Copyright Systems. *Journal of Intellectual Property Law & Practice* 13, no. 10 (2018), 782.

Lewis, A. & J. Taylor. *Sport: Law and Practice*. 3rd ed. Bloomsbury, 2014.

Mc Ardle, D. *Dispute Resolution in Sport, Athletes, Law and Arbitration*. Routledge, 2015.

Mitten, M. *Sports Law in the United States*. 2nd ed. Wolters Kluwer Law & Business, 2014.

Moses, M. *The Principles and Practice of International Commercial Arbitration*. 2nd ed. Cambridge University Press, 2012.

Nafziger, J. Arbitration of Rights and Obligations in the International Sports Arena. *Valparaiso University Law Review* 35 (2001): 357.

O'Leary, L. *Employment and Labour Relations in the Premier League, NBA and the International Rugby Union*. Springer, 2017.

Parrish, R. *Sports Law and Policy in the European Union*. European Policy Research Unit Series. Manchester University Press, 2003, 6.

Selected Bibliography

Paulsson, J. 'Arbitration of International Sports Disputes'. In *The Court of Arbitration for Sport 1984–2004*, edited by I.S. Blackshaw, R.C.R. Siekmann & J.W. Soek. The Hague, The Netherlands: TMC Asser Press, 2006, 41.

Sher, J. When Even Fraud is Not Nearly Enough. Recourse Against Arbitral Awards and Public Policy Considerations: An Anglo-Australian Perspective. *The International Journal of Arbitration, Mediation and Dispute Management* 80 no. 2 (April 2014), 124.

Sumner, C. The Spirit of Sport: The Case for Criminalisation of Doping in the UK. *International Sports Law Journal* 16 (2017): 217–227.

Tweeddale A. et al., Section 69 of the English Arbitration Act 1996-When Fact and Law Collide. *The International Journal of Arbitration, Mediation and Dispute Management* 80 no. 2, (April 2014): 139.

Viret, M. *Evidence in Anti-Doping at the Intersection of Science and Law*. Springer, 2016.

Index

The numbers here refer to paragraph numbers.

Index

Made in the USA
Monee, IL
18 October 2026

66041397R10103